Working with the Mentally Ill

Fourth Edition

ALICE M. ROBINSON, R.N., M.S.

Formerly Director of Nursing Education,
Vermont State Hospital;
Director of Nursing Service and Education,
Boston State Hospital

Foreword by
Walter E. Barton, M.D.

Illustrations by
Jean McConnell

J. B. LIPPINCOTT COMPANY

Philadelphia   Toronto

Fourth Edition

COPYRIGHT © 1971, BY J. B. LIPPINCOTT COMPANY

The first three editions of *Working with the Mentally Ill* were
published under the title, *The Psychiatric Aide.*

COPYRIGHT 1954, BY J. B. LIPPINCOTT COMPANY

COPYRIGHT © 1959, 1964, BY J. B. LIPPINCOTT COMPANY

Distributed in Great Britain by
Blackwell Scientific Publications, Oxford and Edinburgh

ISBN-0-397-54114-7

Library of Congress Catalog Card Number 70-150230

Printed in the United States of America

3   5   6   4   2

Foreword

Through the years, since the first edition of Miss Robinson's book in 1954, then entitled *The Psychiatric Aide*, few works have had greater influence on shaping the attitudes of the psychiatric aide and in improving patient care.

Psychiatric facilities have changed dramatically in the past 16 years and so has the treatment process. Now, acute treatment for mental disorders largely takes place in the doctor's office, in the general hospital, or in the community mental health center. It is possible to handle most mental illness on an extramural basis. There is still, however, an important place for in-hospital management for both acute and chronic illnesses.

Admission to psychiatric facilities is now usually informal or under voluntary circumstances. Chemotherapy is the treatment most frequently prescribed and is increasingly symptom-specific. Every effort is made to maintain the patient's responsibility for self and to enhance his dignity and self-respect while providing motivation for early release from the hospital and return to the community. There is also more emphasis upon rehabilitation and upon health maintenance.

As a consequence of new treatment techniques and new administrative systems, there has been a dramatic drop in mental hospital census. In many psychiatric institutions, the census has been reduced to one half of what it was in the early 1950's. There also has been a change in the type of patients under treatment. There are fewer patients with involutional melancholia, and a greater number of adolescents. There are more cases of alcoholism and drug abuse.

In response to these changes, new sections have been added to this book on drugs, community mental health centers and adolescent patient management as well as on the handling of the needs of older patients.

One of the important changes in mental hospitals is an increasing professionalization of the treatment staff. As the tempo of therapy accelerates, so does the expectation that those providing patient care will be specialists in the management of mental disorders.

Training courses in junior colleges are widely available, offering some of the special training required. Career ladders are developing and are a welcome addition that makes it possible for the ambitious hospital worker to improve his skills and become more proficient in patient management.

Few medical specialties have advanced as far or as rapidly as has psychiatry in the span of time bridged by this book since it first appeared. The years ahead promise an even greater challenge and the excitement of participation in the restoration of the mentally ill to community living.

WALTER E. BARTON, M.D.
Medical Director
American Psychiatric Association

Washington, D.C.
January, 1971

Preface

I would be the first to admit that this revision is long over-due. Societal change since 1964 has been so staggering that it is hard to conceive and, in a sense, digest. Change in our whole societal picture is nothing less than phenomenal.

Since the late nineteenth century, technological progress has far—very far—outpaced human ability to cope with it. The upheaval among young people today can only be called reactionary, and what they are trying to tell us is: "Slow down. Let's look at where we've been, where we are, and where we're going." We of the over-30 generation have been so stymied by this technological onslaught that we have built around ourselves the defense of being "the establishment," with our over-stuffed consciences and narrow, constricted views of what life in the twentieth century is all about.

Close companions to the social unrest of the immediately-past decade are poverty, an increasing population of aged persons, frightening statistics on drug abuse and its partner, alcoholism, and a rise in crime and violence. All of these problems—and their counterparts too numerous to mention—call for a new approach to the care and treatment of multiplying numbers of mentally, emotionally, and societally disturbed human beings. Far greater development of community mental health centers, psychiatric outpatient departments, day and night hospitals, and psychiatric units in general hospitals is needed; along with that development, a serious campaign to recruit mental health workers in all categories, train and educate them, and direct ourselves sternly to an era of prevention and at least a holding operation, must be stepped up.

For these reasons I have added an entire chapter on community mental health centers. I have also added separate chapters on drug addiction and abuse, on the problems of adolescents, and on geriatric patients. I have enlarged the final chapter on "looking ahead." The picture for the psychiatric aide has brightened considerably with support of the ladder concept in education and the "new careers" concept proposed by other writers.

This picture by no means negates the fact that there are still thousands of patients already severely ill enough to be institutionalized. And these patients still need skilled and compassionate care. A dwindling number of professionals in public institutions makes it even more imperative to maintain and increase the number of mental health workers who can deliver that kind of care, particularly to the growing populations of geriatric and adolescent patients.

One appendix found in former editions has been omitted and that is the appendix on classification of mental illness. The *Diagnostic and Statistical Manual of Mental Disorders*, published by the American Psychiatric Association, has become so highly specialized that it will be of little use to the readers of this text. Where the manual may be obtained, however, is listed in Appendix B under "Classification of Mental Illness."

The new title of this book emphasizes that it is meant to serve *all* who work with the mentally ill—including nursing and medical students. The concepts discussed herein are shared by all levels of health workers. However, for the most part, I have continued to use the term "psychiatric aide" in the text, since this is still the most widely accepted nomenclature used to designate those who directly assist with the care of emotionally ill people. There are other terms—nursing assistant, psychiatric technician, mental health worker, community mental health aide, and perhaps additional ones.

Much of the basic content remains essentially unchanged because there are still so many thousands of patients hospitalized in public institutions operated under much the same conditions as they have been for many years. Also, the basic concepts I have presented have not been altered by "societal revolution." Communication, human relations, growth and development, personal defense mechanisms, and humane attitudes will always be a part of the helping life. The *intangibles* of healthful human relationships are *basic*. Antisocial behavior, whether born of loneliness, bitterness, grief, injustice, or other environmental pathology, will still respond to kindness and understanding. This has been true from the beginning of human existence; and it probably will be till the end.

ALICE M. ROBINSON

Contents

Contents

Contents

Contents

Introduction

It was an early summer evening. He stood at the foot of the long, sloping road and looked up at the buildings. They were dull red in the late sunlight, and here and there a light appeared in one of the windows. He thought of the various jobs he had held—laborer, machinist's helper, laundry worker—even bartender. He thought of his children, grown now, and of the problems that he had had to face with them. Now he was beginning a new venture, and not without fear. He remembered the nurse who had interviewed him, wanted to know his experience, his education, and how she had smiled in such a wise way when he mentioned his four children.

He began to walk up the hill. Tomorrow he would start to work as a psychiatric aide.

The Worthwhileness of Your Job

The Problem of Mental Illness

Scattered throughout this country, in every state, are large public mental hospitals. They contain over half a million beds for patients who demonstrate many kinds of behavior which make them different from the average, normal person. Because of their departure from the normal it has become necessary to place them in an environment which offers them numerous advantages—notably, security and understanding—and one in which their progress toward good health can be accomplished more speedily.

Within as short a span of time as the last eight years, increasing emphasis has been placed on the need for and usefulness of community mental health centers. In order to provide for the large segment of our population who need psychiatric help but who never reach the confines of the mental hospital, forward-thinking professionals have advocated and fostered the establishment of community mental health centers, primarily to reach and help people in rural areas and in the deprived ghetto areas of large, overcrowded urban centers. (See Chap. 11.)

The Worthwhileness of Your Job

For many years now the bulk of the load of caring for these sick human beings has been the job of the psychiatric aide. Upon the aide has fallen the burden of daily, hourly contact with the very real, very painful problems of living which these people must endure. Perhaps the enormity of the situation can be demonstrated best by quoting some shocking figures.

There are in the United States approximately 1,600,000 hospitalized mental patients in 527 mental hospitals (264 state hospitals, 43 county hospitals, 40 neuropsychiatric hospitals of the Veterans Administration, and 180 private hospitals). A large percentage of all hospitalized mental patients are in state and county hospitals. General hospitals admitting psychiatric patients number 681. Approximately 617 community general hospitals have separate psychiatric units.*

Each year about 1,000,000 persons are admitted for psychiatric treatment in mental hospitals and in the psychiatric sections of general hospitals. Of these, many are admitted for the second or the third time.

To care for these patients, there are 20,000 physicians, 21,601 registered nurses and 137,000 aids. The need for many more trained personnel in these and other categories is painfully obvious.

Insufficient numbers of personnel constitute only one of the major problems of providing care for the mentally ill. If, ideally, there were enough people to give the specialized, intensified, personal care necessary to restore health in the mental patient, still there would exist economic barriers which in many hospitals, cripple the aide in his job to the point of hopelessness. Often, there is not enough clothing; sometimes, the food and the serving of food are inadequate; frequently, the buildings are old (and sometimes hazardous); the furniture may be bare and dingy and hard. The aide works with

---

* Facts About Mental Illness (1969 fact sheet), National Association for Mental Health, 10 Columbus Circle, New York, N .Y., 10019.

the patient, day in and day out, sometimes without instruction and guidance, often knowing that he is not doing his best.

This is not true everywhere. In the past 60 years tremendous strides have been made in the improvement of care for the mentally ill. Each year new hospital buildings are constructed, more workers recruited, new forms of treatment discovered, and new steps made toward making the general public aware of its obligations toward caring for the mentally ill.

Throughout all this runs the problem of status for the psychiatric aide. Foresighted, intelligent leaders have long recognized the courage, the service and the worthwhileness of the aide's job. They have known the recovered patient who says that an aide helped her to get well; they have seen untidy wards where the lone aide works all day at a discouraging task; they have watched aides lifting and bathing and changing older patients with gentleness and humor. They have depended on aides to help them with treatments, to watch over their patients at night, to comfort patients whose relatives have not come on visiting days. These things and many more have made recognition of the aide an actual fact and have prompted medical, nursing, aide and lay leaders to campaign for better salaries, to set up educational programs, to formulate better screening policies for hiring new workers and to consider the status of aides in relation to other workers.

The History of Mental Illness

Mental illness began as time and human existence began. We know that it occurred even during prehistoric ages, because there is evidence of crude operations upon the skull in even the earliest excavations. Probably, these first tribes banished the afflicted one from the group, leaving him at the mercy of storms, cold, wild beasts or starvation. In prehistoric times, the very preservation of life was man's major responsibility, and the tribe member who could not care for himself must, of necessity, have been cast out.

As one surveys the course of mental illness throughout the development of civilization, one cannot help noting the ups and downs of attitudes toward such suffering. In early Biblical times, temples were built in idyllic spots where special

150 Years

forms of treatment were provided, not unlike our present-day music therapy, hydrotherapy, and occupational therapy. In the "Golden Age" of Greece, this tolerant attitude prevailed, and famed Greek physicians even attempted to separate mental illness in diagnosis from the common physical illnesses.

With the downfall of these lavish early empires, however, attitudes also took a turn. For many hundreds of years, in fact, up until the middle of the 18th century, the mentally ill were treated as witches and evil ones, cruelly beaten, chained, tortured and burned. Medieval man looked upon the mentally ill person as one possessed by evil spirits, devils and demons which must be driven from his body by the most drastic means. Only the religious orders offered a haven, but so few found their way into the monasteries that the unjust toll in human life was appalling. Read the reference item by Sister Bernadette Armiger (see reading list, Appendix B) for a fascinating account of one 40-year period in the "care and treatment" of the mentally ill in this country.

Unfortunately, the term "Bedlam" is often used, even today, to describe mental hospitals. The name comes from an incorrect pronunciation of Bethlehem, a town in England, where in the early 16th century an insane asylum was established. Here, on Sundays, people came from miles around, paid a small pittance and watched the wretched inmates chained to the walls on straw mats, much as one would go to the zoo on a Sunday afternoon to watch the animals. The picture was essentially the same in asylums in other parts of Europe and in the jails and the almshouses of this country.

Toward the end of the 18th century some prominent names appear with the advent of a distinct reformation in the care of mental patients. It is not nearly so important to remember the names as it is to recall that they were people who worked with a real feeling of kindness, pity and humility. They were people who wanted to help the so-called insane and to make the public aware that such a thing existed in society, that it was a sickness, not a sin, and that it was the responsibility of the mentally well in the community to improve the conditions under which the unfortunate patients lived.

The French physician, Phillipe Pinel, was the first of the real reformers. He is famous for "removing the chains from the mentally ill." It is hard to realize that today, 150 years later, we are still removing restraints from our patients!

No account of the progress in care of the mentally ill could be given without mentioning Dorothea Dix. Miss Dix was not a physician or a nurse but a community member who began her working career as a schoolteacher. Her teaching brought her face to face with the disgraceful living conditions in the jails and the poorhouses, and she soon recognized that many of the persons so "put away" were mentally ill and not petty criminals. With an unusual ambition and zeal, she set out to inform the public, particularly members of government, of the undesirable facilities and methods in common practice at that time. Her efforts toward reform, strikingly enough, accomplished much improvement in many institutions in the United States. Not only were improvements made, but money was raised for the establishment of new institutions.

Following closely on the heels of this reform movement credited solely to Miss Dix, another name becomes important —that of Clifford Beers. Clifford Beers, hospitalized for some time with mental illness, recovered sufficiently to write the book, *A Mind That Found Itself*, and to be instrumental in the founding of the National Committee for Mental Hygiene in 1908. This committee, now active in all parts of the world, has worked constantly, since its beginning, toward educating the public to the problems of the mentally ill and toward improving the conditions in mental hospitals. Now known as The National Association for Mental Health, it has, in recent years, focused particular attention on the problems of psychiatric aides and has been instrumental in the improvement of their working conditions and status.

Sigmund Freud, who first formulated the theories of psychoanalysis and brought to light the tremendous importance of the effect of growth and development on one's mental and emotional balance in later life, was a Viennese psychiatrist whose greatest work was done in the 1920's. His theories were particularly concerned with sexual development, and, for the first time, this taboo subject was placed before the public in such a way that healthful progress followed. Actually, one of his greatest contributions was a subtle one—that of prevention—for with much greater knowledge of the period from infancy to adulthood, the bringing up of children achieved its rightful importance in the prevention of later mental illness.

The historical development of the special forms of treatment used in mental illness and the prevention of mental illness will be discussed in Chapter 7.

Kinds of Facilities

The facilities available for mental patients have undergone changes, also. Many years ago, and even today in some rural areas, when a person became mentally ill, he was cared for at home. The community looked upon him as "queer" or "odd" but harmless. Community members fostered his protection and were sympathetic toward his family. Only when the sick person became harmful toward others was he placed in an institution. Today, several kinds of facilities are offered for his protection and return to health.

The large public mental hospitals fall into 3 main categories: state, veterans, and city or county hospitals. A small percentage of public care is given in "children's units" and in research hospitals. More and more general hospitals are opening psychiatric wards. Although there are still a number of small private hospitals, they are expensive to maintain and expensive to patients.

Supplementing these facilities, especially in the area of prevention, are the clinics which each year take care of thousands of persons on an outpatient basis, and the "halfway" or rehabilitation houses which "bridge the gap" between the psychiatric hospital and the community. (Chaps. 10 and 11.)

Kinds of Workers

In all of these facilities many people work around the patient in attempting to help him get himself well. Psychiatrists, nurses, aides, psychologists, occupational and recreational therapists, social workers and a myriad of maids, porters, kitchen help, clerks, and maintenance personnel, all, in some way, contribute to patient care. The psychiatrist, with a wealth of special training behind him, is ultimately responsible for the physical and emotional health of the patient. He prescribes the treatment for his patient and leaves directions for care with nurses and aides. The nurse, too, offers leadership for other workers, sees that the doctor's orders are carried out and watches the comfort of patients as to eating, sleeping and clothing. She learns early the secret of knowing her patients well, so that she may sense impending periods of disturbance, the onset of feeding difficulties, the need for religious counsel, or countless other daily problems confronting patients.

The clinical psychologist contributes to the care of patients primarily through the use of tests which are an aid to the psychiatrist in determining diagnoses and subsequent plans for treatment. Most commonly used in mental hospitals, and those with which the aide may come in contact, are the Binet-Simon intelligence test for measuring the level of intelligence for a human being; the Rorschach test in which a series of prepared ink blots are shown to the patient who, in turn, tells the psychologist what he sees therein; and the "T.A.T." (Thematic

Apperception Test) in which a series of vague photographs is shown to the patient, and he is asked to tell a story about each picture.

Occupational therapy *includes* recreational therapy, and the two should not be separated into two distinct services to patients. Anything in the way of physical or mental activity which is directed toward keeping patients in a world of reality can be classified as occupational therapy. At the present time, the use of industrial therapy as another offshoot of occupational therapy is assuming more and more importance. Where once patients were made to work, or, at least were *expected* to work, they now work under competent supervision at jobs which they choose and for which they are best suited. The aim of industrial therapy is the preparation of the patient for going back into the community as a working, productive individual. Occupational therapists work with patients under a doctor's prescription which is specific for each patient. In a number of hospitals today, notably in the Veterans Administration hospitals, patients who are considered ready for it are employed in organized hospital work-programs and are paid for their work. Some patients go daily to jobs outside the hospital—for which they are paid ongoing salaries—returning to the hospital at night and on weekends—unless, of course, they choose to go home for weekends.

The social service department plays a very important part in the life of the hospitalized mental patient. The social worker is the closest link between the patient, his home, his family and the community. Most patients, except those who are very, very sick on admission (and even those sometimes!) have financial and domestic problems with which they need help. There may be little children who must be cared for; a payment may be due on the television; the husband may be alcoholic; there may be an aged mother left alone in the apartment. Whenever possible, the social worker sees the sick person and/or his family as soon after admission as possible and offers great relief to the patient by taking care of immediate needs such as those mentioned above.

As psychiatry moves forward and we are faced every day with masses of people needing help, and there are few personnel to offer help, we are beginning to utilize all specialized personnel in doing therapy with individual patients or groups of patients. "Doing therapy" can mean many things, but essentially it means making direct, frequent, personal contact with a patient or patients in friendship and trust in order to help them to find their way out of the darkness of illness and into the light of health.

What Is Your Job?

In the middle of all this, standing with the patient, is the aide. What is the aide's job? This is a momentous question, one on which much time has been spent by many people. The job differs somewhat according to the policies and the philosophies of the different institutions, but there are many basic parts of the job which are inevitably the same. Most large mental hospitals house the patient according to his illness. For instance, a newly admitted patient or a readmission goes to an admitting building; the patient who has been ill for a long time (the chronically disturbed, the untidy, the chronic patient who is "hospital-adjusted") lives on a so-called chronic service; the older patient goes to the senile or geriatric unit; the patient who is physically ill with a heart condition, leg ulcers, pneumonia, etc., lives in the infirmary or the medical surgical building where he can receive bedcare; the patient who receives special treatment such as a new "Drug Project," is housed in a small unit which is equipped and staffed for the specific type of treatment. A relatively new concept of admitting and housing patients is the "unit system" whereby patients are admitted—regardless of their age, diagnosis, or behavior—

according to the geographical location from which they come in the state or municipality the particular hospital serves. This is viewed as a forward step by its advocates since it eliminates unit "reputations"—senile ward, disturbed ward, infirmary, and the like. The aide works in any or all of these areas, and in each one his job differs somewhat. One thing creates an all-important sameness—*every one of the patients is mentally ill.* The job demands, first, then, that the aide care for patients with this fact *always* in mind.

The second greatest part of the job is learning to know each patient—his name (and what he likes to be called!); his habits in relation to life's basic needs—eating, bathing, dressing, sleeping, elimination, medications, and the outstanding indications of his general behavior.

The third major responsibility of the aide's job lies in making an attempt to *understand* the patient so that the reasons for certain behavior patterns become clear and so that the knowledge of these reasons can be used constructively in promoting recovery and lessening the possibilities of prolonging the illness. This understanding begins with common sense. For example, Mary K. cannot sleep and paces the floor at night because the metal grille outside her window is loose and rattles in the wind. Jack gets very angry every Sunday because that is visiting day, and he never has visitors; he stands in a corner of the day hall and watches other patients and their visitors. Betty lies on the floor next to the pipes all day because she has on only a thin dress, and the ward is chilly.

From such intuitive understanding should come the stimulation to attend staff conferences where everyone can discuss more fully some behavior that seems to be unreasonable. Frank fights every time he has to take a shower because he is terrified of electric shock treatments, and at the other hospital, a shower was always given before shock. Marian carries a bag of odds and ends in her arms and becomes very upset when

an attempt is made to take it away from her. Marian wanted
a baby of her own but was never married. In her mind, the
bag is a very real baby.

Besides staff conferences, there is much to be gained by
reading and by asking to be included for inservice classes.

All of these things contribute to a beginning understanding
of behavior and are a major part of the job because they make
the job easier. Lack of understanding on the part of the aide
as to why a patient behaves in a certain way creates impatience, frustration, and disinterest in the job.

There are two other major parts of the job which are not
mechanical—that is, not done with the hands and the feet.
The aide should know what is expected of him, and therefore,
from the beginning he should *ask questions*. Finally, and by
far the most important, the aide must become aware of interpersonal relations and what that term means. The newborn
baby soon becomes aware of other people in his small world;
as soon as he is aware of them, he reacts to them in one way
or another—actually, he either likes them or he does not,
and he acts toward them accordingly. Throughout life this
goes on. We meet new people and we feel something about
them; we communicate with them by our actions and with
words, and we have an effect on them. The aide meets and
works closely with many patients. Frequently, he does very
personal things for the patient, such as bathing and toiletting
him. It is of paramount importance that he be aware of himself in terms of the effect of the patient on him, and of how
he is affecting the patient. If we do not like someone, we do
not want him around us, and we especially do not want him
doing something for us. The aide should know when a patient dislikes him, and until he has an opportunity to find out
why and whether or not something can be done about it, it is
wisest, if at all possible, to let some other aide give that particular patient the attention that he needs. On the other hand,

if a warm, friendly relationship exists between a patient and an aide, the benefits that can be extended to the patient are limitless.

This awareness of feelings means looking at yourself critically, which is not easy. However, being aware of one's problems is only half the battle. *Doing* something about them is the healthy, mature way to make progress. How often, when discouraged or angry about something, do we take out our feelings on others? And how often can we admit it and attempt to control it?

The aide is the one person who maintains constant contact with the patient for sustained lengths of time. Therefore it is the aide on whom the patient depends for a secure environment and proper physical care.

Physical care brings to mind the tangible aspects of the job. These are concerned with daily living—the aide must know if or how the patient slept; he must make sure that the patient eats and drinks; he must make sure the patient is properly toiletted, bathed and dressed; he helps with housekeeping—clean floors, walls, bathrooms, and beds are a vital part of a healthy environment; he must know the elementary signs and symptoms of physical illness—fever, chills, vomiting, bruises, swelling, and so on—and must be able to report them quickly and accurately; in line with this, he must be familiar with the more commonly used ataractic drugs, and particularly, he must be alert to the undesirable side-effects; he must be able to make beds, help with special treatments, make routine checks of equipment and laundry, keep accurate count of his patients, weigh them, take them for walks, to movies, and a dozen other errands all of which are important to the safety and the comfort of his patients.

In all these tasks he learns to respect his co-workers, to *work with them,* to help the nurses in their special jobs, to keep the doctor informed about his patients, and to add to the work being done by occupational therapy by continuing diversional activity on the ward.

All kinds of emergency situations add to the job. The aide may be asked to stay with a suicidal or a disturbed patient; he may have to help transport patients in the ambulance from one area to another; he may be asked to help with a patient in the dental clinic; he may accompany the social worker in bringing an outpatient into the hospital. In some hospitals, aides help count and sort laundry, or are responsible for patient's clothing and valuables, or must serve and give out meals. Whatever the job, the aide will do well to develop a healthy philosophy about his job and to use it as his primary guide in caring for patients.

A Philosophy for Psychiatric Aides

Throughout this chapter, much has been said which indicates a thorough respect and admiration for the psychiatric aide. This is the direct result of lengthy observation of aides working, day by day, with mentally ill persons. As in any other kind of work, there are all kinds of people who venture to work in a psychiatric hospital. Up until recently, the screening process for hiring amounted to little or nothing, and the quality of workmanship and the resulting meager care of patients spoke for itself. Frequently, petty criminals, alcoholics, neurotics and shiftless individuals went to work in mental hospitals because no place else would have them; the hospitals hired them because they needed help so desperately that anyone who could walk and talk was better than nothing. A few well-meaning, hard-working, humane people worked alongside them, hating the brutality, the neglect, the slovenliness that inevitably was the result of ill-educated, uncaring help. The doctors and the nurses (if there were nurses) ignored the deplorable situation because they felt helpless to combat the seemingly insurmountable problem.

Today, most hospitals employ a competent personnel director, and the aide applicant must possess certain characteristics and attributes before he is accepted for employment. The salary, the prestige and the interest of the job are attracting more and more people who have humane principles in their hearts, who are interested in progress and in their fellow man and recognize a sickness as such and want to do something about it. Urban hospitals are employing more and more college and university students, both men and women. Everywhere, throughout the country, the impetus is more and more toward education for the psychiatric aide, either in on-the-job inservice programs or the more formal educational programs of 12, 18 and 24 months, some including undergraduate college work and others even an undergraduate degree.

With improved conditions, aides still fall, generally, into 4 main categories: (1) the person who has tried many jobs, perhaps has raised a family, and feels that a job as an aide caring for the mentally ill will offer security and interest and also will be a contribution to the community; (2) the student, who needs to work while going to school or desires experience which will offer better preparation for his chosen field of work; (3) the "drifter," who knows that the mental hospital is a "soft touch" for a while, or feels protected in an environment of sick people, or is domineering enough to want to work where he can assert himself with people who, for the most part, cannot or will not fight back. The term "drifter" is used here because, fortunately, those who fall into this category are becoming fewer and fewer and are the ones who are not dependable, who do not accept their share of the load, who are always late or absent and are responsible for many of the "accidents" and "falls" which happen to patients; and (4) the person who wishes to make a career of being a mental hospital aide, who starts out with this in mind and takes pains to prepare himself for the job.

The Worthwhileness of Your Job

In order to take care of the mentally ill, one should always keep in mind that the patient is *sick*. Even though he may seem to know when he is being mean and ornery, the fact that he does so, even though it is quite clear that the desire of those around him is to help him, *indicates* that he is sick. The patient is a person who has lost control, who becomes not only depressed but *very* depressed, who becomes not only angry but *very* angry. The patient is sick because he has lost faith in those persons who are closest to him. He feels that he is alone, has no one and nothing to lean on. He needs someone who will care about him, care what happens to him, who will talk to him even when he cannot talk to them, who will help him to learn all over again to eat, to sleep, to dress himself, and to realize that the real, the outside world is a better place to be. He needs to know and be with another human being who can accept him, who has accepted himself and made adjustments accordingly.

It is this recognition of sickness and the inherent needs of sickness that must be constantly kept uppermost in the mind of the aide and, in fact, of any person working with and for the mentally ill patient.

Introduction

From the beginning he liked his work, but he was frightened. The tall tales told by his co-workers added to his own former ideas about "crazy people" and made it difficult for him. He sometimes found himself laughing at the wrong things, or criticizing without first trying to understand. A kind, experienced aide, working with him, helped him to meet these first minor crises. He slowly became aware that mental patients are people with the same kinds of needs and problems that he had—only more so! He slowly became aware of his own importance to the patient, and he began to want to do more and more. He read much, and he inquired about signing up for some of the educational programs at the hospital.

It's Not What You Do, It's How You Do It

Communication and Human Relations

Communication might well be defined as a meaningful *contact between people* which is either positive or negative and can be either verbal or nonverbal. Communication skills are developed through concentration on the following: the words we use, the manner in which we express words, and the bodily movements with which we accompany words. Communication is vitally essential to human beings. People probably could exist without communication, but such an existence would be deathlike. The mental patient who is unable to communicate is also unable to get better.

It is true that in everyday life when we are capable of expressing our feelings honestly and securely and when we can "talk out our problems," we become more peaceful within ourselves and can live in better harmony with our fellow men.

The reason that the patient usually arrives on the admitting ward "acutely ill" is the fact that he has not been able to communicate to anyone *the way he feels,* and tensions have built up as the result of increasing emotional conflict. Usually, after he has been started on a drug which the physician feels will help in his particular problem, his most overt *symptoms* disappear. However, although the symptoms may subside, the causative conflicts and problems are still very much within the patient. Should the drug be discontinued at this point, he undoubtedly would revert back to the sick behavior which necessitated his initial hospitalization. (Occasionally, patients improve and become more accessible to staff simply by virtue of being removed from a troublesome environment into a more secure one.) At any rate, he is now "available" for healthful communication, and at this turning point for the patient the aide needs to know something of the skills of communication. His degree of skill in this area may help the patient to accept his hospitalization, have confidence in staff members and feel comfortable with necessary ward routines, loss of personal privacy, and acclimation to other patients.

Most people have the ability to communicate to the extent that they "get along" from day to day, many of them without too much difficulty. But *inadequate* communication is responsible for most of our problems from the slight friction which can exist between two people, all the way up the scale to world-shaking problems such as war.

What are some general principles which the aide can apply in order to improve his own skills of communication?

"Know Thyself." Although no one could ever completely live up to that precept, it is possible for people to look more closely at themselves and their relationships with others. It is not an easy task, but in the long run it becomes a highly rewarding experience. Through increased understanding of one's own behavior, one is better able to understand the behavior of others.

The psychiatric aide, in his relationships with patients, might well ask himself these general questions: (1) How do patients respond to me? (2) What are my feelings about mental patients? (3) What kind of judgments do I make about patients? (4) How do I react to these feelings and judgments? (5) Why do I particularly like or dislike certain patients? Talking over such questions with a co-worker, instructor or supervisor will sometimes bring to light valuable information which we might not be able to perceive in ourselves.

Understanding Others. As he begins to understand himself, the aide has made an important step in his attempt to understand others. *The basis for understanding is knowledge.*

The aide may carefully *observe* his patient's behavior patterns, what he likes to do and with whom, among the other patients, he spends most of his time. He may question the head nurse or the doctor about the patient's life before hospitalization. He may make it a point to meet his patient's visitors—family and friends—and then contemplate the interaction taking place. He may spend extra time with the patient drawing him out through objective conversation.

Verbal Communication. The use of words and colloquialisms in such "objective conversations" with patients should be in accordance with the patient's capacity to understand. *How* words are expressed has a definite effect on the attitude with which they are received by the patient. There are many ways in which a patient can be requested to do something! Such a request—regardless of whether it is firm, gentle, coaxing or humorous—will be well received by the patient if it is made with *sincerity* and with implied understanding.

Symbolic and Literal Statements. Often, we find ourselves thinking that the very sick patient is "talking a lot of nonsense." *This is a dangerous precept,* as illustrated by the following true account:

A patient on the admission ward, hospitalized only a few days, had been very agitated, seemed to be actively hallucinating and had been expressing many religious delusions. She seemed to be really preoccupied with religion, frequently quoting passages from the Bible. On this particular day, she had been pacing up and down apparently growing more and more apprehensive. Finally, she wandered down to the door of the nurses' station and said to the young nurse in charge: "Would you look at my right eye? Is there anything wrong with it?" The nurse, who was busy, did get up and look, but said, kindly enough: "Eleanor, please don't bother me—your eye looks fine!"

The patient returned several minutes later and asked the same question.

This time the nurse's voice held a slight edge:

"Eleanor, your eye is fine. If you don't feel less upset pretty soon, we shall have to put you in a room by yourself for a while."

Not long after this, the patient was put in "seclusion." Ten minutes later, an aide who glanced into the room noted with horror that the patient had gouged out her own eye.

On the way over to surgery, the patient kept repeating: "If thy right eye offend thee, pluck it out!"

There are those who will call this a far-fetched example, and perhaps it is. The nurse would have had to be "psychic" to have picked up the implication contained in the patient's anxious question about her eye. But it does serve to point out that often what a patient says *on the surface* has much deeper meaning.

Two other examples come to mind which are far lighter in impact, but they also emphasize the danger of not paying attention to patients:

An aide on evening shift was engrossed in talking with the supervisor in the office. A long-term schizophrenic appeared at the door and said:

"Bill, will you come to my room? There's a goat under my bed!"

The aide grinned and replied, sure, he'd be down soon.

Within the next half an hour, the patient returned twice

with the same complaining request. Finally, upon seeing that his patient was becoming quite agitated, the aide went to his room. There *was* a real, live goat under the bed!

The third example probably has happened more than once.

Once, I had a very obese patient who had been hospitalized for several years. To my knowledge, she had not been off the grounds for at least a year. One day, she came into the office and said: "Did you know I was pregnant?" Suppressing a smile, I replied that I didn't know it and told her not to worry about it.

For several weeks she kept telling me this, and I kept giving her the same response.

One night at about 11 o'clock, I got a frantic call from the aide on her ward, and rushed up just in time to help deliver a healthy, 7-lb. boy. (There wasn't time for the doctor to get there!) I shall never forget her, lying there—a big grin on her face—chortling, "I told you so, Miss R. I told you so!"

It is really so difficult to judge what is fact and what is fiction that it is always wise to *listen carefully* and when there is any feeling of fact, intuitive or otherwise, to pursue the subject further.

Nonverbal Communication. From the minutely raised eyebrow to the strident, athletic walk, the influence of bodily movement has vast implication in the development of communicative skills. Relatively speaking, interest in nonverbal communication, or bodily expression, has only recently become the object of intensive study by workers in the psychiatric field.

For the psychiatric aide, it is particularly important. He may say one thing to the patient and feel another. For example, an aide comes on duty in the afternoon and begins to visit with each of his patients as he makes his initial rounds. He comes to a man who is unshaven, his clothing soiled with dried food particles, his hands filthy and his arm in a dirty sling. "Hello, George!" says the aide, "You're looking fine!" In reality, the aide is repulsed and is thinking, "You disgusting slob. That so-and-so on first shift should have cleaned you up!" The aide is feeling revulsion toward the

Nonverbal Communication

patient and anger toward the first shift aide. Patients have an uncanny sensitivity to our nonverbal expressions. In the above situation, the aide may "give himself away" in several ways: he may step back a bit when he first looks at the patient; he may put his hands in his pockets to avoid shaking hands with the patient, should the patient happen to offer; his jaw may clench; he may frown; his voice may be overly loud. Although he may not know *why*, the patient will certainly sense that the aide is reacting negatively to him, and he will feel insecure. How much better for the patient if the aide could comfortably say: "Why, George! Still having trouble eating with that arm, huh? You'll feel better if you come along with me, and we'll get you cleaned up!" Because he is, at one and the same time, telling the patient that he is messy, but that he cares enough about him to help him clean up, the aide is maintaining the patient's self-esteem and yet releasing the valve a bit on his own feelings.

Positive nonverbal communication is perceived more easily. However, it is just as important that the aide be aware of positive bodily expression. As he seeks to overcome negative reactions, so he may seek to develop positive reactions.

Before closing this section, attention should be drawn to the inestimable importance of observing, reporting *and* attempting to understand the many nonverbal messages which patients convey to aides through their actions. An aide became very puzzled at the nightly ritual of one of her patients. She would examine every inch of her bed and the area around her bed; then she would completely undo the bed, shake the sheets and make it up again, tightening it at all 4 corners so that there was only space enough for her head to go through at the top; next she would put on a pair of long cotton stockings and completely cover her head with a nightcap. After all this ritual was completed, then, and then only, would she crawl into bed, being careful not to disturb her handiwork.

On top of all this, she would get up several times during the night and go through the same procedure. Obviously, she was getting very little rest. The patient steadfastly refused to answer any questions regarding her strange behavior, so the aide brought her problem to the next inservice class. Several members of the class made suggestions, and then one ventured the idea that maybe the patient was afraid of mice and imagined that they would get on or into her bed. Four mousetraps were obtained and placed beside each leg of the bed. The aide, without referring to the patient's fears, matter-of-factly pointed out the mousetraps and left the patient preparing for bed. After carefully inspecting the traps several times, the patient climbed into bed without any of the usual ritual and slept well for the first time in many nights.

More often, a patient's nonverbal communication is not that obvious. The psychiatric aide should be aware of the subtle signs of increasing depression: the puzzled expression of the patient who misidentifies someone; the self-abuse implied by constant pacing; the panic which sometimes precedes a disturbed episode.

It is not difficult to develop a skilled awareness of bodily expression and its meaning. Smiles, frowns, a handshake, a pat on the back, positive or negative shakes of the head, salutes, crossed fingers and a multitude of other simple gestures have become such a vitally important facet of human communication that they can be observed easily wherever there are people.

The Importance of Attitudes

For the aide who considers his job seriously and sincerely wishes to help his patients, attitudes toward mental illness assume tremendous importance. In considering the problem of healthful and nonhealthful attitudes, we must discuss not only current attitudes of the general public but also the attitude of the aide himself. It is relatively simple to tell someone else what to do; it is next to impossible to tell him how to do it. The *how* of doing things involves most emphatically the *personality* of the individual doing the job. Every personality is different, even as every person is different. How we affect others in our dealings with them, and how we are affected *by* others involves many parts of us which make up a total picture of our personality.

There are many available definitions of personality. In fact, whole books have been written on the subject. Let us consider an everyday evaluation of the meaning of personality. Briefly, it involves physical, mental and spiritual development in relation to the social sphere in which one lives. Appearance, voice, manner, control, general intelligence, ability and warmth are the main parts of the over-all personality. Warmth should be especially considered, since it involves efforts to move toward others in understanding and sympathy, with humor and relatedness. We judge another's personality quite simply by the way in which he affects us. A limp handshake can discourage respect rapidly; a loud, strident voice arouses feelings of annoyance toward the speaker. A clean, neat appearance attracts praiseworthy attention, whereas a soiled and rumpled appearance, though it assuredly attracts attention, arouses critical comment and evaluation. The person who laughs too easily and too much, or becomes quickly and exceptionally angry is viewed with some anxiety by his associates.

The aide, whether or not he is aware of it, uses his personality as his first and most important tool in dealing with patients. His ability to size up the personality of others is a secondary but important tool also. Thus, it will be brought out again and again in this text that knowing the patient and the important expressions of his behavior is the first task of the aide. Not only is it important to know a patient and what to expect of him in terms of behavior but also to understand one's own feelings about such behavior. This involves forming an attitude.

In early times, as mentioned in the previous chapter, people shunned the mentally ill, punished and ridiculed them and were mostly concerned with getting rid of them. The basis for this attitude was fear born of ignorance. They did not know the why and wherefore of insanity and thus were afraid of it. Today, such attitudes still prevail but are not acted upon in the same drastic manner as in the past. As we grow more and more toward an urban way of life, the tendency is still to "get rid of" the patient, since we cannot let him wander the streets and cannot tolerate his peculiar ways. But not by burning him at the stake! Instead, he is placed in an institution, and in many cases simply forgotten there. People still view mental illness in terms of "loonies" and "nuts" and speak of the mental hospital as the "nuthouse" or the "insane asylum." Newspapers describe an escaped mental patient as a "violent madman." Magazines, movies and television have attempted to aid the cause of caring for the mentally ill by showing pictures of scrawny, bearded patients chained or strapped to beds, others lying nude in filthy wards, and still others dressed in rags staring from behind large iron bars. This has aroused some public action toward improvement, but not enough. Although now the trend in publicity is toward pointing up modern facilities and treatments, the average layman still has little or no understanding of mental illness. Many view it as a degeneration, feeble-mindedness, or moral weakness. They fear for the person who works with mental patients, often saying to the aide, "How can you stand it, working day after day among all those crazy people?" The general concept is one of danger. The new aide, although he may not admit it, is afraid that he will be physically assaulted. This primary attitude cannot be condoned, yet neither can it be criticized. It is the direct result of a lack of knowledge about mental illness. Spending time with patients under the helpful supervision of a competent, experienced aide will dispel this fear more quickly than will classes and books. Patients are, first of all, people, and they are people in need of help. A mentally ill patient is sensitively aware of the feelings of those around him, and it is this sensitivity that makes it so necessary to develop healthful attitudes.

Sympathy and Empathy

What kinds of attitudes are most productive as a basis for successful relationships with patients? Feelings of superiority, authority, ridicule and physical power must be weeded out. In place of them can be substituted *sympathy*—not an emotional gush of pity, but a sincere, humble kind of sympathy that recognizes that mental illness knows no selection. In other words, "There, but for the grace of God, go I." An aide, working with old people, recently remarked: "I often think, as I bathe them or help them to the bathroom, that it might well be my own mother or grandmother I am caring for, and I find it easier to be patient because of that thought." One cannot hear a patient cry out without feeling some of the anguish behind the cry.

Empathy is another important attitude, not so easily achieved as sympathy. One has to *experience* feelings and responses in order to empathize. A nurse who has had children of her own can *share* the experience of labor and delivery with a mother; an aide who has controlled his own alcoholism or drug addiction can give much to the alcoholic or drug-addicted patient; an aide who has been divorced by her husband may well be more aware of the anguish the rejected patient feels.

Actually, most of us, at one time or another, experience some of the emotional misery with which patients cannot cope.

This may account for that immeasurable quality of "heart" that some aides have toward patients which is not acquired in the classroom.

It is possible to remain somewhat detached when the feeling is that of sympathy. On the other hand, empathy is more involved because: "I *know* how you feel." As with sympathy, empathy can be overdone and, consequently, is not healthy for either patient or aide.

Hopefulness

An attitude of *hopefulness* is essential. One of the greatest dangers the aide must guard against is allowing himself to despair of his patients' getting well. This is sometimes extremely difficult, for no illness is more baffling and discouraging than mental illness. A feeling of defeat is very quickly communicated to the patient, and when the patient loses hope, the battle is done. His chances for recovery slide further down the scale. Every year new methods are developed for the treatment of mental illness, and it is important to keep in mind the fact that many so-called hopelessly ill patients have been redeemed simply because someone had *faith* in their ultimate chance for recovery.

Kindness

Gentleness and courtesy indicate an attitude of *kindness*. Most mental patients are sick because they have been unsuccessful in relating to people and have thus become the victims of unkind actions. The aide, substituting for parent, friend or teacher, can restore self-respect to the patient by his thoughtfulness. Such thoughtfulness should be a part of everyday activities with patients. With a loved patient, it is not difficult to be kind and considerate. With the disliked or constantly irritating patient it becomes a matter of controlling the feeling of dislike and perhaps even changing it by taking more time to be gentle and courteous about lifting, or dressing, or talking. This involves endless patience, and the development of patience is an art which means making a sincere effort toward understanding behavior. Losing patience with a mentally ill person, yelling at him, pushing him, or striking him is *never* excusable. Not only is it inexcusable, but it can undo, in a very short space of time, any good which has been done by many days of hard work.

Realism

An attitude of *realism* in relation to a patient is extremely important to the process of helping him to get well. Thus, the aide must not allow himself to agree with or uphold a patient's bizarre ideas or behavior, since this merely strengthens such ideas in the patient's mind. However, this does not mean that his behavior cannot be tolerated, or that his behavior can be ridiculed, since there are times in the course of the illness when it is quite necessary for the patient to talk or "act out" the inner workings of his mind. It is necessary to remember always that no matter what the patient says or does, regardless of how vague or unreasonable or eccentric it may seem, it *means something* to the patient. Often the aide represents to the patient his only contact with the real, outside world. Thus, an attempt should be made to maintain, at all times, a realistic attitude toward the patient's sickness, his hospitalization and his contacts with others.

Respect for the Patient

A person's self-respect is the backbone of his personality. With it he can stand up straight, face the world, and contribute his share to the good of mankind. For many reasons, mental illness often involves the loss of self-respect. Not only is it frequently a cause of the illness, but sometimes it is the result of the illness. The stigma attached to being in a mental institution very often is communicated by thoughtless relatives, employers and friends, and the patient may be deeply ashamed of his "nervous breakdown." Thus, it is of the utmost importance to rebuild carefully with the patient his self-respect, and to gain his confidence and trust, first in us and ultimately in himself. The aide can develop an attitude of *respect* for the patient as a human being who is temporarily unable to care for himself. Respect involves such things as appreciating the patient's need for privacy, his need to have possessions he can call his own, his need for attention and need to be understood.

Whatever attitudes the aide develops toward his patients, he also carries with him into the community. No end of good will toward mental illness and the mental hospital can be built if the aide communicates to his own circle of friends and associates sound, healthful attitudes such as those outlined above. The role of "unofficial public relations officer" should be assumed as quickly as possible, since it is one of the important obligations of the aide's job. People may be hesitant toward accepting a healthy viewpoint in exchange for a fearful one, but as with the theory of water wearing away a stone, every drop, or every word, counts.

Meeting the Patient's Emotional Needs

A discussion of attitudes leads most naturally into a discussion of emotions. A person's emotional status is conditioned by the *attitudes* of those around him—his family, friends, co-workers and acquaintances. Feelings and emotions are so closely related as to mean practically the same thing. However, emotion generally is understood to indicate a *stronger* response to attitudes. The two terms will be used similarly in discussing the needs of the patient for an understanding of his reactions to people and things.

Lack of Emotional Control

Nearly everyone experiences, at one time or another, a period of lack of emotional control. That is, we can get very tired and discouraged and can become so depressed about it that our work, our relationships with our families, and many other things can suffer. Or maybe we are constantly irritable, looking everywhere for arguments and generally creating an unpleasant atmosphere for ourselves and others. Fortunately, we can usually work through these periods of uncontrolled emotions without needing professional help. Maybe friend, or husband, or co-worker lends a hand, but mostly we ourselves become aware of our emotional difficulty and its cause, and attempt to eliminate it, so that once again we can function adequately at work and at home.

The patient is in the hospital because his emotional status became so disturbed that the usual remedies failed and he needed professional help. During our growing-up years many emotional needs arise in us. Some of these needs are satisfied normally; others may produce in us frustration and hostility because they have not been satisfied. Whatever the outcome of the need has been, it has had a very definite effect on our individuality—our responses to everyday situations. New situations call forth the emotional responses that we have had previously to similar incidents. Thus our patients, meeting new situations in the hospital setting, are going to have certain emotional responses. The aide must be aware of what these responses are likely to be since more often than not, they will be exaggerated, and the patient will need help in dealing with them.

Fear

The most common, basic emotional responses to needs fall in the following divisions: fear, anger, grief, hate and love. It is not by chance that fear is the first of these to be listed.

It's Not What You Do, It's How You Do It

Fear is the element which is always present for the mental patient, and an element which conditions most of his activities and the activities of those around him. Even the "seasoned" or long-term metal patient is fearful; he may be afraid of the dark, or of his fellow patients, or of personnel, or of loneliness. For the newly admitted patient there are these fears plus dozens of others: he has heard tales about mental hospitals, it is all very new and *strange* to him, he may be afraid of the food, he may be afraid to go to bed among strangers whom he thinks may kill him. Some mentally sick persons have never been hospitalized in *any* kind of hospital before. The process of admission may add terror to the initial dismay of being brought into a mental hospital. He is faced

Fear

with all sorts of necessary procedures—a physical examination, routine bathing, dozens of questions, the removal of personal possessions. He meets, in a short space of time, any number of people whom he has never seen before. No matter how kind they are, how patient, he may still feel, perhaps as a result of his sickness, that they are all eager to do him harm.

There are two general responses to the emotion of fear. The patient may strike out in an attempt to eliminate the fear, or he may withdraw. As an obvious example of the latter we can recall the hospitalized soldiers during World War II who, at the sound of any explosion, great or small, threw themselves under their beds and crouched in real terror until reassured and led into the open by a comforting aide or nurse. The average mental patient who withdraws does so by avoiding other patients and other personnel, often sitting in the corner or remaining in his room, refusing to eat, sometimes even refusing to move. This pattern of withdrawal, when the direct result of fear, demands much patience on the part of the aide who is responsible for the patient's well-being. A quiet, friendly, consistent manner does two things: it can build the patient's confidence in the aide *as a person,* and it can demonstrate to the patient, by example, that he will be free from the harm that he so desperately fears. This type of reaction to fear on the part of a patient may result in his being neglected. He gives no obvious "trouble," and, on an active, busy admitting ward, we must be careful that he does not get lost in the rush.

On the other hand, a patient who reacts to fear by striking out may do so in a number of ways: he may be talkative, extremely noisy, destructive, or assaultive. He may pick on other patients, keep the ward disturbed at night, or refuse to wear clothes. Sometimes we interpret this behavior as mean and stubborn, but, keeping in mind that the patient is sick and afraid, we can recognize his need for reassuring human presence. We should avoid, as much as possible, the use of physical force in dealing with this type of conduct. If, ideally, we could provide the constant presence of an aide who inspires trust, upon whom the patient can heap all of his expression of fear, we could divert his energies into productive, healthful channels. We could let him help us clean, or engage him in active ward games where he could become a part of the ward group. Since this is, frequently, not possible, it is the aide's job to recognize the mounting activity and to report it to the nurse or the doctor.

Anger

Anger as a response to an emotional need is also fairly common among mental patients. Anger usually follows frustration. That is, a person wants something, or wants to do something, and, at every turn, is stopped. After so long a time something has to give, and usually it is a person's patience. Anger can be vented by verbal or physical abuse toward someone or something outside of oneself. It can exist in varying degrees from a sullen, withdrawn silence to proportions which may even end in a tragedy such as murder. Of the five responses listed previously—fear, anger, grief, hate and love—anger is probably the most dangerous, since there is less control present when a patient responds angrily to a felt need. He may shout, cry, threaten, or be destructive. *As long as no harm is done to other persons or to things*, it is sometimes helpful to allow such expressions of anger, because in this way he "blows off steam." When the outburst is over, often he can be dealt with much more practically than if interfered with during the outburst. In a chronic disturbed service one often sees a patient walking up and down the porch loudly making all sorts of accusations—sometimes toward specific persons, sometimes toward the world in general. An hour later, the patient can be observed making beds or sweeping the hall and is easily accessible for conversation. On the other hand, if such an outburst is handled by immediate banishment to seclusion, or is counterattacked by anger from the aide or the nurse, it will continue and grow in intensity.

Anger is also frequently directed inward and, if such is the case, may be accompanied by feelings of hate toward oneself. Patients who react in this way are sometimes self-abusive, that is, they may pull out their own hair, scratch themselves, bite nails down to the quick, or beat themselves in the head. The self-abusive patient needs constant attention and needs to be kept busy. Anger, whether directed outward or inward, should be *redirected* by the aide. If a punching bag is available, it is a good remedy for men *or* women; so is bowling, hammering boards together, moving beds, or scrubbing walls. When the initial "heat" of the anger has been spent, it is well to determine the object of the anger and to pass on such information to the patient's doctor.

One further point regarding anger is that a patient's anger

Anger

is seldom directed toward the aide *personally*. Often, it will appear this way because the patient may express verbal and even physical abuse toward a particular member of the staff. This is almost always displacement (Chap. 4) and should not be viewed as a personal affront.

Grief

Grief is defined by Webster as mental pain, sorrow, distress. It is a baffling problem to both the patient and those who care for him, because it is usually a deep-seated and subtle kind of reaction. The depression accompanying grief is most frequently the result of the loss of a loved one by rejection, desertion or death, although any *failure* can produce depression. Until a substitute is offered for the loss or the failure, the patient suffers a very real, physical ache, and he may be suicidal. The person who has lost someone he loves very much is slow to accept any kind of substitute, for he is plagued by memories of happier times, and each memory brings forth new feelings of loneliness and despair. It is important that the person who is sick with grief be made

Grief

aware of things outside himself and, if he is a religious person, church activities and close contact with his chaplain will help. Although suicide will be discussed thoroughly in Chapter 9, it is well to remember that thoughts of self-destruction may be uppermost in the mind of the patient who is grief-stricken. The patient should be carefully observed at all times, *without his being aware of it,* and he should be encouraged to participate in group activities as much as possible. The sincere friendship of the aide can provide him with enough stimulus to help him to become aware of other people and things. One thing that is unsuccessful with depressed patients is the attempt to be bright and cheerful. When a person is deeply depressed, *nothing* really helps. This is very well brought out in the film, "The Faces of Depression,"* in which a recovered patient discusses his feelings while in the depths of depression.

Love and Hate

Contrary to popular belief, love and hate can exist together and frequently do. These are two of the strongest emotional responses of which human beings are capable. Love, particularly, is a dominant factor throughout life. In the normal course of events, we love our families, our friends and husband or wife. We are also capable of deep spiritual love, love of objects and, most important, self-love. Love of another person implies many things—tolerance, understanding, companionship, respect, loyalty, all of which spell *giving*. Many people are not capable of giving and lead self-centered, narrow lives, frequently missing the happiness contained in sharing things with someone else.

The large percentage of mental patients are sick because of some difficulty in a love-relationship. A person's early rela-

---

* "The Faces of Depression" is available on a rental basis from the Geigy Pharmaceutical Co.

tionships with his parents, for instance, have tremendous influence on his success or failure in life as he matures and attempts to function as an adult. The aide should remember that he almost always represents someone in the patient's past life toward whom the patient has felt either love or hate or both. Thus, he should not be offended if a patient dislikes him; likewise, he must be careful that a patient who *does* like him does not become overly dependent on him or overly attached to him. It is important to maintain a stable and consistent attitude toward patients, since the patient is seeking a way to get well, and it is our responsibility to offer him a realistic path to follow. A patient does not become overly attached or overly dependent without encouragement. If we allow ourselves to become involved with patients through any sort of strong emotional tie, we are only creating more problems for a person already so beset with problems that he

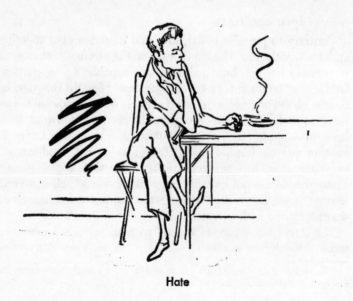

Hate

cannot function within the community. Often, we do not recognize such overattachment, and it is always wise to divide time fairly evenly with patients, and to seek advice from others who know the patient.

Hate, like grief, presents a challenge because it is a subtle reaction. Hate is usually well controlled and masked by all kinds of deceptive behavior. Hate, or hostility, is expressed in many different ways—rejection, withdrawal, sarcasm, overly sweet helpfulness or flattery and in the manipulation of one staff member against another. Hate, being a nonproductive factor, must, like anger, be redirected. It can gradually wear itself out and be replaced by feeling and activity which work ultimately for the common good.

It is tempting in a discussion of emotional responses to include happiness and satisfaction, but these do not present *needs*, and we are concerned with so many *problems* that we simply rejoice in the sharing of positive emotional responses.

Attitudes and responses to attitudes have been discussed in a general way. There are many other patient reactions which take place each day. If the aide is prepared to meet the basic, dominant attitudes presented, he will also be able to meet the varying *degrees* of these dominant attitudes. With so many patients to care for, he must meet them with economy and tact, with interest and responsibility.

The Over-all Ward Attitude

In line with the intangible forces with which we have been dealing in this section we need to explore the over-all atmosphere—the *feeling tone*—of the ward.

To the patient, his ward may not be his *home*, but it is the nearest thing to home during his hospital stay. Thus, for a period ranging anywhere from one or two weeks to a number of years, he eats, sleeps, possibly works and plays and generally carries out the activities of *living* in a specific ward. It may seem like home to him, or it may be a bedlam which will make him sicker. Much of how he feels about his ward is going to depend on the aides who take care of him and take care of his environment.

As one walks through a large mental hospital, one becomes aware that certain wards, although similar in many respects, differ greatly as to the behavior of patients and the appearance of the ward. For example, a visit on two disturbed female wards in the same building reveals the following: they have the same ward plan, same number of patients, the same number of personnel. We are likely to find one ward quiet, pleasant, the radio playing softly, and the patients engaged in various activities, such as games, or dancing, or stacking linen, or cleaning. In the other ward, we may find seclusion rooms filled, the ward littered, patients angry, sullen and disturbed. Wherein lies the contrast? Further investigation will disclose that the aides on the first ward are busy with patients, working together, making frequent contact with the head nurse and the doctor; they are consistent, interested and responsible. On the second ward, the aides may be sitting in the office, or bellowing at a patient to clean up the mess, quibbling among themselves as to who is boss or who is responsible, fearful of the doctor and indifferent to the head nurse. Patients know all these things and feel insecure. They expect from the total hospital setting protection, love and help in getting well. They have every right to expect this from us, and it is our obligation to provide them with this service.

The ward atmosphere depends greatly on the attitudes of the assigned personnel. The influence of the aide's feelings about his patients, his job and co-workers is often underestimated. For example, there is the value of personal appearance. An aide who does not pay strict attention to his own personal hygiene is not likely to be particularly interested in the personal hygiene of his patients. Cleanliness and order are only a *part* of creating an emotionally healthy atmosphere. Aides who get along well with one another, who recognize leadership and are sympathetic with each other's problems will extend the same qualities toward patients. The response of the patients to such a harmonious attitude will make the job easier in the long run. Difficulties which arise between two people (supposedly working together toward the common good of helping patients to get well) should be discussed either by the two, or with a third interested but objective person. If this does not solve the difficulty, a request for another assignment may be the answer. It is an accepted fact that many harmful developments can result when personnel do not get along well together. For example, the disturbed patient can readily sense tension when the aide comes into his room to minister to him. The aide may have too much to do, too much responsibility, because the two aides working with him went off to lunch together. He is uneasy and angry, and his tolerance level is lowered. The patient is looking for stability and comfort, and when it is not available, his own anxiety increases. He does not feel protected or belonging—two very important elements at this particular time in his illness—and he may become panicky.

The depressed patient may be ignored entirely by personnel who are annoyed with one another. The food on his tray may go uneaten, and his feelings of loneliness and guilt will increase. The aides, concerned with their own problems, cannot be concerned with his. This is primarily selfishness; even though we cannot entirely ignore our own feelings, we can try to remember that, during the hours on duty, the obligation is toward helping a person whose feelings are much more overwhelming than ours, a person whose ability to cope with his unhealthy feelings is much less than ours. He is sick.

In some hospitals, this theory of the importance of personnel attitudes and their effect on patients has been developed to the point of *prescribing* attitudes. In relation to particular patients, the physician actually prescribes an attitude of firmness, or joviality, or sympathy, or consistency—whatever the particular situation demands, and personnel are expected to administer such attitudes much as they would administer any other specific treatment.

Time off duty and some more appropriate place should be utilized to settle interpersonnel difficulties. To add such difficulties to the patients' load may be the straw that breaks the camel's back!

Introduction

From the books he read in the hospital library, from ward conferences and from conversations he had with patients, he began to realize that what happens during the early part of life has a profound influence on one's later years. That he understood himself better was a natural result of this study. Many times he came off duty tired and baffled, wondering if he was doing the right thing, trying to fit two and two together. Of one thing he became certain, patients did get better and did go home. It made him question, "Why do some people get sick, and others don't? It seems to me that many times their past has been very similar. Are there differences we don't know about?" On his days off, around the neighborhood, he began to watch the behavior of children more carefully. He knew that from them he could learn a great deal.

—————————————3

What You Need To Know About Normal Growth and Development

Why People Get Sick

It is only in recent years that understanding of the processes of mental illness has begun. There is still so much to be learned that we frequently work in a maze of theory and guesswork. One thing is certain beyond doubt and that is that mind and body are inseparable, and what affects one is bound to affect the other to greater or lesser degree. This is easily seen in the general hospital patient who has a serious operation and has all kinds of emotional reactions before and after. The patient is always fearful, tense and sometimes irritable. Patients with inoperable cancer may become very hostile toward those most dear to them, and thus bewilder relatives and friends. Likewise, the mental patient presents many physiologic changes in the progress of his illness. If he is overactive, he may become dehydrated and undernourished, or his skin may break down and form ulcers or a rash; if he is underactive, he may develop constipation, bedsores or circulatory changes. Aides have often remarked in class how amazed they are when patients with marked behavior difficulties change and become so well behaved when hospitalized in the infirmary building because of a broken leg, or pneumonia, or an operation. It is of vital importance that those working with the mentally ill never forget this close association between mind and body; too often we ignore the physical and tend to belittle it, sometimes neglecting to pay attention to symptoms which could develop into serious physical illness.

If more were known about why people get sick, intensive programs could be developed for prevention and eventually there would be fewer mental patients. Recently, much emphasis has been placed on the process of interpersonal relations and its very profound effects, and as more is learned about what goes on between people, the job of caring for persons with maladjusted personalities will become easier. Certainly everything that is said and done between the aide and the patient during daily contacts is extremely important. The more the aide becomes aware of this interrelationship, the better he will be able to function with his patients.

Why is so much importance being placed upon this factor? Simply because most mental patients are sick *because they have failed to relate successfully to a person or persons!* This failure *plus the person's reaction to the failure* are the beginnings of mental illness for the majority of hospitalized patients. This is known as *functional* mental illness; that is, no physical cause can be found to explain the abnormal behavior.

Other reasons why people get sick are easier to understand and cope with. For instance, the organic diseases which may produce a psychosis; if there is a tumor of the brain, or if there are changes in the blood vessels of the brain due to old age, there are mechanical methods of treating the illness (i.e., drugs, surgery). If a patient has had syphilis for a number of years, we know that certain damage occurs in the brain and the spinal nerves, and emotional and physical impairment will result. There are specific, mechanical treatments for syphilis, also. These are *organic* conditions.

A small percentage of patients are the mentally retarded who fall into two general categories—those with psychosis and those without psychosis. Mental deficiency is in most cases the result of either injury or illness at birth or during infancy. A few are believed to be the result of hereditary factors. Because of their initial low intellectual capacity, these people are unable to cope with the demands of society and must live in special communities where they can receive care and learn simple tasks. Those who are mentally retarded and psychotic soon manifest unacceptable behavior (most commonly destructiveness, extreme rage reactions, and assaultiveness) and have to be placed in the mental hospital for their own protection and for the protection of others.

Of the largest group—the functional mental illnesses—the least is known. Every patient is sick as an individual and he cannot be clumped into any special group. He is sick for reasons all his own; he reacts to his sickness in his own way; he gets well in his own way. Those who care for him must care for him *as an individual.* If he is "one of the herd" he cannot get well. "There is never enough time" is the cry. But we should take time. We should recognize the things about the patient that are specifically individual and capitalize on them—*use* them to help him get well.

Often it has been said that if there were only enough people caring for the mentally ill so that there might be one person for every patient, there would be no more incapacitating mental illness. Thus, every volunteer, every relative, every doctor, nurse, aide and other kind of worker who can establish a healthful, positive relationship with a patient is easing the load a little. Many an unsung nursing student, affiliating for only three months, has helped an individual patient toward that much-desired goal—an acceptable place in the community. As a matter of fact, the nursing student has a unique opportunity to help individual patients, because she is not also expected to carry the bulk of the task of housekeeping and administration along with her obligations for good patient care. With careful guidance, she has an opportunity to apply learned concepts with her patients.

Functional mental illness is baffling. It has its roots deep in the patient's past, and the roots are strong because they have grown through the developmental years. The open wound of functional mental illness may be healed, but the scar will always remain. People are not yet able to accept mental illness, and it is hard to find a job, to marry, to become a harmonious part of the whole. The patient needs everyone's help as he slowly and painstakingly rebuilds his very foundation.

From Infancy to Adulthood

As we look around in the world today, we do not find it a very happy place. Daily newspapers are filled with war news, crime, divorce, prejudice, sickness—all the things which indicate an inability on the part of the human race to cope with its own progress. Things move too swiftly, and it is a constant and difficult struggle to adjust each day to the process of living. People do find happiness, but it is a relative thing, dependent on background and immediate circumstances, including other people. People seek happiness as though it were something which, when achieved, would last throughout life. This is not the case, but it is possible to make adjustments which keep life a worthwhile thing and make us productive individuals.

Since we are dealing with the care of persons mentally ill, it is important to know something of the ways of children— how they grow and develop into adults. Every day, we run into problems with patients which are a direct reflection, if not a repetition, of the problems of childhood.

The person who begins life under the optimum circumstances of comfort, contentment and opportunity is rare

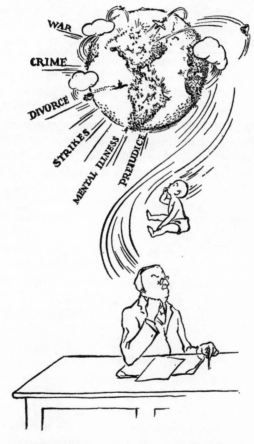

The child faces a world of problems.

indeed. He is a person who will ultimately make a real contribution to those around him and to the world at large. It is important to remember that *the common denominator of healthy growth and development is love and security*. Upon these two factors can be built a physically and emotionally mature person.

In order to determine how growth and development take place in an individual and what problems arise during this process, it is essential that we work toward a common and acceptable understanding. In the Introduction, Freud is described as having made a tremendous contribution to medicine and psychiatry because he outlined a pattern of growth and development which has helped parents, teachers and everyday people to understand themselves and their children better. Although many people cannot accept strictly Freudian thinking, the emphasis placed upon his theories in the field of psychiatry makes it necessary for all those working with the mentally ill to have at least a beginning knowledge of growth and development as he outlined it.

Because the subject is vast and complicated, only the bare essentials will be included here. However, the student is advised to study further in order to enlarge upon what will be presented in this text, since probably no other subject is as important in reaching an understanding of mental patients. Beginning with the premise that a greater maturity is distinctly necessary in mankind, we must begin to interpret the structure of personality.

Constitutional Factors

First, it is important to recognize the influence of what are called *constitutional factors*. We know that the instant a baby is born he begins to develop a personality, for it becomes necessary for him to react to a multitude of new situations and other human beings. The world begins to make demands on him immediately and continues to do so throughout life. The physical or constitutional characteristics which influence this personality development include body build, texture of hair, color of eyes, and general intellectual capacity, or brain structure. We know that we *inherit* these things from our forebears. We also know that we do *not* inherit bad tempers, moodiness, the habit of drinking, excessive neatness and other personality characteristics. It is granted that parents may have any one of these characteristics, and that the child will also; but it is quite logical to admit that, because of the constant contact with such a parent for a number of years, *imitation* is surely going to take place. Under ordinary circumstances, children live with, depend upon and *follow the examples* that their parents set for them. The inheritance of certain physical characteristics is important in the building of personality, but not nearly so important as the effects of the outside world of reality upon an individual.

In describing the consecutive stages of normal growth and development a terminology will be used which can be recognized by any kind of worker on the mental hospital team. Therefore, it is important for the aide to become familiar with these terms so that he can benefit from discussions concerning patients and the treatment of patients.

Phases of Growth and Development

Oral Phase. The first phase of development described by Freud is the oral phase, which lasts usually until the end of the first year. The very first activities of the baby are very much concerned with his mouth; hence, the term "oral." Hunger pains bring to the infant one of his first sensations of unpleasantness, and for the first few weeks he is solely concerned with feeding, sleeping, and warmth. It is generally considered best that mothers nurse their babies because it is so extremely important that the baby have frequent and close contact with the mother. Since it is not always physically possible for the mother to nurse her child, some babies must be bottle-fed. Although this *will* provide the baby with the proper nutrition, it cannot be a substitute for the security and the warmth of contact with the mother. Thus, mothers are urged to hold babies while they feed them and to pick them up and fondle them frequently during these early weeks. This is the *normal* course of development.

Problems arise when, for one reason or another, the baby feels himself alone and unwanted. It may seem far-fetched, and actually babies do not specifically think, "I am unwanted!" but they most assuredly have vague feelings of discomfort when seldom held and loved, when left to lie for long periods of time, often uncomfortably, without being turned or picked up, when allowed to go hungry beyond their first hunger pangs. We know from the study of many patient histories that children who were treated this way as infants grew up as insecure, withdrawn, hesitant people who, more often than not, were unable to cope with the difficulties of living and became sick.

Under what circumstances do babies feel alone and unwanted? Sometimes, for very practical reasons the mother cannot provide healthy care for her baby. She may be ill, she may have to work, she may have several other children. It is also possible that she did not want the child and does not love the child. If this is the case, no matter how hard she tries to overcome these feelings, the baby will sense them. He will not sense the exact feelings, but only that something is not right in his environment. The baby should have his mother, her comfort and her satisfaction of his basic needs as much as possible during the first year. Many of the feeding problems encountered with patients are, at least in part, the result of an emotionally unhealthy atmosphere during the oral stage.

Anal Phase. The second phase of development is known as the anal phase. It lasts, roughly, from the end of the first year until the beginning of the third year. Up until the start of this phase, the child has been completely dependent. Now he is asked to accept regularity and responsibility, specifically in terms of toilet training. Because our culture has so rigidly forced such matters into the background of daily living, this phase is probably the most important in leaving a mark, one way or the other, upon personality development. Human elimination is looked on as a necessary evil, something "dirty," not talked about, but nevertheless essential to life. Therefore, the process of toilet training becomes, to many parents, a dreaded and disliked ordeal. Theoretically, if parents were less *concerned* and impatient about helping their children to develop proper habits of elimination, if they consistently support, love, and endure this period with the child, few, if any, problems arise in this area.

Many mothers feel that toilet training should be accomplished in two months or less. After all, it is a fairly simple procedure—why doesn't the baby catch on? One observes the usual time of a child's bowel movements and, just before they are due, places the child on the toilet, carefully indicating that this is the proper way. Since children are barely beginning to comprehend language at this point, the mother must indicate by gesture, by patient support and by her warmth what she expects from the child, and should show him that she is pleased when he successfully accomplishes his task. If this plan is followed through regularly for several months, the whole process of toilet training can be completed by the end of the second year. The child may soil himself occasionally, but, for the most part, he will accept his responsibility, knowing that this is what his parents expect of him and that this is a way he can please them.

On the other hand, all sorts of severe problems can arise

when parents become overly concerned during this period. If there is constant tension between parents at this time, if the mother becomes angry and impatient with the child, if she punishes him when he soils himself, the child is going to feel bewildered and puzzled and sure that his mother does not love him. He can react in many ways, some of the most common being to withhold the contents of his bowel, to soil himself purposely, or to smear the products of his elimination. The latter is most alarming to the mother, as it is later to us when patients do exactly the same thing! It is important to understand that this kind of reaction on the part of the child is a form of resistance to the mother because she has disappointed him. He finds this way of getting even. So our patients, when things get tough and they feel incapable of adjustment, may revert right back to this behavior, since it has produced results for them in the dim past.

The advice given mothers in the face of this problem is applicable to patients also. First, that such behavior must be accepted, that disapproval must not be expressed. Instead, one cleans up the mess and gives the patient clay, finger paints, even ordinary cold cream that he can smear. If the patient soils himself it will not help him to tease him or speak harshly to him. If we do, we are establishing ourselves in the same role that his mother took, and he will respond by the same kind of resistance—soiling himself again and again. Instead, he can be showered, dressed and kept occupied with a group of patients. Patients who demonstrate this type of behavior during their sickness need to be toileted frequently until they have learned, once again, to accept the responsibility of their own routine.

Genital Phase. The third, or genital phase, lasting from the third to the sixth years, is mainly concerned with infantile sexuality. It is this phase of the Freudian concept that is so hard for the average person to accept. This is quite understandable, since it is difficult in our present sociologic background of development to accept the fact that small children have any ideas about sex. The subject of sex has been assumed to be something that is "not nice," and certainly not to be talked about among "nice" people. It is obvious that sex plays an all-important role in the scheme of things, and certainly, since this is true, we should be aware of the process of sexual development, as we are aware of the other factors that go into building the mature individual. The mistake of overestimating the erotic or *romantic* aspects is one of the chief reasons why people resist the idea of infantile sexuality. We must remember that the child is constantly seeking *pleasure*. When he fondles various parts of his own body, he is not aware that he is masturbating, or that he is doing something unacceptable. It is only when parents become very upset and tense about it that it assumes abnormal flavoring for the child. Up until that point, he is only following the normal pattern of being curious about his own body, and discovering that from it he can derive pleasurable sensations.

SEX EDUCATION. Many, many problems arise during the genital phase. For purposes of this text, only four major problems will be discussed. The first is the important subject of sex education for children. Sex education *by the parents* should be given in a patient, matter-of-fact manner, as soon as is necessary—that is, with the child's first question concerning sex. And *each question only* need be answered. It is likely that the first questions about sex are going to appear when the mother becomes pregnant again. Children's questions should be answered in simple, straightforward language. If the child does not get straight answers, if he is told that talk of sex is bad or naughty, or if he is actually punished, his feelings of guilt and fear are going to create problems in relation to sex throughout his life. As seen in their records, so many patients have had sexual difficulties leading to illness, or at least contributing greatly to the illness, that the subject must be considered carefully by those who are going to care for them. Guilt and fear about sex resulting from incomplete or distorted knowledge of sex probably are two of the major reasons for divorce in this country. Curiosity about sex, as well as certain sexual activity in children, must be regarded by parents as a normal part of growing up. The handling of this part of development should receive no more emphasis than the handling of other factors in growth and development.

MASTURBATION. The second important subject is that of masturbation, since masturbation is frequently a symptom of mental illness, and the aide should understand rather than criticize or be uncomfortable about it. It is generally accepted that any child will seek pleasurable stimulation from his own body during the very early years of his life. It is necessary to keep in mind that this is a *normal* outcome of his curiosity regarding himself. With certain people, masturbation may continue (but not excessively, which indicates a far more serious problem) until a marital relationship has been established. *Masturbation is not physically harmful in any way* but *does* become a problem when a conflict sets in. Such a conflict springs from an unhealthy attitude on the part of parents, teachers and others toward it. Children are severely punished, severely reprimanded, teased, threatened and frightened by parents regarding masturbation. When this happens, the child becomes confused, unhappy and ashamed, and rather than discontinue the habit, he may indulge in it to excess. He may feel that his parents do not love him or understand him, and he will seek pleasure from this new activity. Moreover, he will hide and do it secretly, which will increase his guilt and isolate him even farther from his parents. This vicious cycle can be avoided by a wise and tolerant attitude on the part of the mother and the father and by a program bent toward diverting the child's interests and energies. Parents should spend more time with the child during this period; they should make sure that he is not alone any more than is necessary; they should offer him intriguing games and play-mates until such time as he is able to drop the habit by him-self. Masturbation on the part of mental patients deserves the same attitude and the same effort toward diversion on the part of the aide. Frequent vigorous activity, cleanliness, and mixing with other groups of patients are effective remedies for the problem with the mentally ill adult.

OEDIPUS COMPLEX. The third major problem is involved with what Freud termed the Oedipus complex. The term stands for the emotional attraction that a child between the ages of three and six feels toward the parent of the opposite sex. Normally, it occurs at the time of the child's first experi-ence of being away from home, that is, his entrance into school. Simply stated, little girls fall in love with their fathers, and little boys fall in love with their mothers. Understandably, jealous and hostile feelings toward the parent of the same sex exist at this time. It is a difficult period for both children and their parents and, unless delicately handled, can result in a permanent attachment for one or the other parent. Such a result may be followed by inability to marry, simply because the child, grown into an adult, never finds a person who suffi-ciently represents the loved parent. Occasionally, one or the other parent will ignorantly (or willfully) encourage such a relationship, actually enjoying it and never releasing the hold on the child. Thus, there are men who live with and are devoted to their mothers, who do not marry and seem quite content to have things that way. Likewise, many a daughter keeps house for her father until such time as he dies. Usually, she is left without the prospect of marriage simply because she has devoted all of her time to her father.

The manifestations of the struggle are the same as in any love triangle. The child wishes to obtain the sole attention of the loved parent and talks of wanting to marry him or her. A boy may be very jealous of the father, resenting his attentions to the mother and even striking the father in moments of intense feeling. In discussing this in class recently, an aide told of his own son who, for a period of time during this phase, kept locking him out of the house each time he went out. Fortunately, he had handled the situation with understanding, did not get angry, and allowed the boy to continue the practice until eventually he stopped. Usually, if parents recognize this phase in children and are tolerant about it, the child will redirect his feelings onto other persons. His activities at school are a great help, because he becomes interested in his little pals and his teachers, and gradually the intensity of the feeling for his parent disappears. A patient of about 35 in group therapy continuously talks of getting out of the hospital so that she can marry her father and have babies. She is an example of an unresolved Oedipus complex, and only by careful reorientation and subsequent awareness of the root of her problem will she be able to see the unacceptability of this and the necessity for more normal adjustment.

SIBLING RIVALRY. The fourth problem to be outlined appears when another child is born. This is referred to as sibling rivalry—a sibling being a brother or sister who is an offspring of the same parents. A child quickly becomes aware that the mother is pregnant; in fact, often before others in the household notice it. When told that a new brother or sister is due in the near future, he may become vaguely uneasy, although he may not understand why. When the new baby arrives, he is bound to become jealous and to feel unwanted, because the parents necessarily must spend more time in caring for the infant. He wants to get rid of the new child, and he may become very resentful toward the mother because she is the cause of his jealousy and, deep down inside, of his guilt for feeling jealous. He will resort to all kinds of methods to regain his mother's attention. It is during this period that most difficulties of speech appear, that children develop loss of appetite, or they return to the thumb-sucking of the oral phase. Parents who really love their children will recognize what these things mean and will make sure that the first child receives ample attention.

During later stages, this problem of sibling rivalry may arise again and again. Many patients tell of an older or a younger sister or brother who is especially attractive or bright, who received all the parents' attention and "always got everything." Sometimes, a child is constantly compared with this "superior" brother or sister in such a way as to develop in him a severe inferiority complex and eventual lack of interest toward bettering himself. Often, the oldest child is given too much responsibility for the care of the younger children and is not permitted to enjoy the normal relations and activities of his own group. Parents must try to divide equally among their children attention, love, and responsibility. When this is done, there will be fewer patients who hate the world, withdraw into themselves and refuse to make friends with anyone.

Latent Period. From six to ten years of age, children go through the latent period. Not too much has been determined about this particular phase of development, since it is relatively quiet in respect to activity. Children are busy, interested in school and other learning experiences, but they are not interested in the other sex, form gangs, and generally do not seem to take life too seriously. There are the beginnings of an urge to be independent of the parents, and many children at this time begin to form ideas as to their future life work.

HOMOSEXUALITY. One process worked through during this phase is homosexuality, and only during this period is it looked upon as a normal part of growth and development. Homosexuality, or an attraction for one of the same sex, is seldom openly set forth by children but expresses itself in their obvious antagonism toward the opposite sex. Little girls play at being mothers—they sew, cook, and play with dolls—and think of little boys as wild and dirty and mean. Little boys, on the other hand, look upon girls as sissies and generally useless individuals. As mentioned above, this phase is considered as normal and becomes a problem only when the child's emotional development stops at this level. However, when this occurs, and homosexuality continues as the individual's method of sex expression, it is an indication of a number of more deep-seated problems. Homosexuality among mental patients can become a serious problem for aides, and for that reason it will be discussed more thoroughly in relation to patients in Chapter 5.

Puberty. This is the phase during which certain profound physical changes occur, and along with them, specific personality changes. This is a particularly trying and significant phase for girls, since it includes the onset of menstruation, which can affect women in many ways until middle age, or menopause. Other physiologic changes take place, and with them a growing awareness of sex and feelings toward persons of the opposite sex. Children need the close support of their parents during this phase, and it is particularly important that the changes involved be fully explained to children and understood by them. This is especially true with girls, since so many old wives' tales exist in relation to menstruation. Among women patients three things are important for the aide to know: (1) the need for cleanliness, (2) a need to fathom the particular ideas of each patient regarding menstruation and (3) the awareness that many women patients become highly disturbed during the period of menstruation.

Adolescence. The final phase of growth and development before adulthood is that of adolescence. The adolescent phase is the most difficult to understand and to manage on the part of both children and parents because it represents the transition from child to adult, with all the implied responsibility and independence. Actually, adolescence is the last period of dependency for the human being in the normal sense of the word, and for both child and parents it involves giving up a close attachment.

English and Pearson* have outlined four tasks of adolescents as follows: (1) he must decide on a vocation and prepare for it; (2) he must effect ultimate separation from his parents; (3) he must bring about a satisfactory relation with the opposite sex; and (4) he must effect a completion of his personality for mature responsibility. In the face of these four major tasks, the adolescent responds according to his progress in growth and development so far. If he enters adolescence inadequately prepared, it is more or less his last chance to make of himself a productive, mature individual. The opportunities are many, and most children who have ridden out serious problems (with their parents' help) in earlier life will adapt satisfactorily. However, those who do not succeed stand the bad chance of becoming seriously maladjusted, nonproductive individuals who, more than likely, will become the responsibility of society before too long, either as delinquents or as mental patients.

This evaluation of the growth and development of human beings from infancy to adulthood has been, of necessity, very brief. Countless problems arise during each phase, and the aide will discover, as he begins to know each patient better, that each has had his own particular problems and has adjusted or has failed to become adjusted accordingly. It is hoped that the material which has been presented will stimulate the reader to delve further into the subject, for the better

---

* English, O. S., and Pearson, G. H. J.: Emotional Problems of Living, 3rd ed., p. 278, New York, Norton, 1963.

we know our fellow human beings, the better prepared we shall be to help them in their time of need.

The Levels of the Mind

The *meaning* of personality and some of the ways by which we judge it have been discussed briefly in Chapter 2. With some understanding of growth and development, we should now move to an understanding of the three basic components of personality, outlined originally by Freud. Again, we use his terminology, because the psychiatric aide will hear and read the terms in his daily work. It is interesting to note that *Ego, Id* and *Superego* are also being used more and more frequently in movies, magazines, and everyday conversations.

The initial way to comprehend the three basic parts of personality is first to acquaint ourselves with the "levels of the mind"—the conscious, the subconscious or preconscious, and the unconscious. An iceberg is a very simple and yet striking analogy. The greater part of an iceberg is submerged beneath

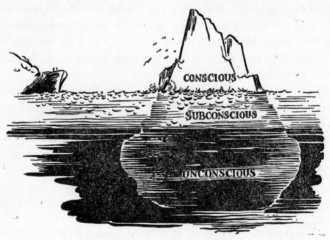

The Levels of the Mind

the surface and thus is invisible. The smallest part of an iceberg shows quite clearly, and this we liken to the *conscious* mind. *The conscious mind contains all of which we are immediately aware, through all of our senses, at any given moment in time.* One is aware that it is cold or hot, that one is hungry or not hungry, that it is quiet or noisy, and so on. All these things present themselves to our conscious minds. Responses to emotions, memories brought forward—in essence, one's state of *being*—are registered in the conscious mind.

Almost immediately, these things become memories, but memories which, in most instances, we can recall easily. Returning to the analogy, these memories are not deeply submerged, and on closer inspection, they can be "seen" when we look for them, just as more of an iceberg's bulk can be seen as it is approached by a ship. This, then, we call the subconscious mind. *The subconscious mind contains memories which are relatively easy to recall.*

By far the largest mass of an iceberg is so far beneath the surface that it cannot be seen. Similarly, the bulk of our memories (experiences) are deeply hidden in the unconscious. *The unconscious is a vast storehouse of remembrances which are not recalled easily but, most importantly, do influence our behavior.*

Of the three levels of the mind, the unconscious is the most important for the very reason that it influences our behavior. Much of our behavior we do not understand could be explained if we could delve into the unconscious and sort out memories. Every experience and reaction to experience which we ever have had is recorded there, and it would be safe to say that the memories living in the unconscious basically are unpleasant memories. The miracle of the human mind protects us from such a vast sea of memories which we probably could not tolerate were we aware of them all of the time.

Since the unconscious is really somewhat of a "problem child" and has an uncanny way of not only playing tricks on us (slips of the tongue, forgetting something very well known, like a familiar telephone number), but also creating serious difficulties, an example will be given to illustrate its remarkable influence.

A young woman comes to a psychiatrist with a typical phobic complaint. She has become increasingly afraid of small, closed spaces and finally has had to take a leave of absence from her job because she cannot ride the elevators to and from her office on the 23rd floor. After several interviews, the psychiatrist elicits the following story from her:

When she was four years old, her father, whom she adored, came home from work one evening and accused her of having done something she had not done. In a fit of anger (probably about something else), he locked her in a closet for an hour. While in the dark, stuffy closet, she kept thinking to herself, over and over again: "I hate you! I hate you! I wish you were dead!" Of course, this is a common reaction of small children, particularly when they are punished unjustly, but at the time they are thinking these things, the reaction is a very real and important one.

Not long after this episode *and before the child and her father had had an opportunity to resolve their difficulty,* the father had a coronary and died.

Immediately, the child repressed the memory of her expressed death-wish toward her father, and it lay buried in her unconscious for years. Her tremendously guilty feeling of responsibility for her father's death became fixed in the memory of the locked, small closet and emerged as a phobia of small, closed spaces.

In a few more sessions, the psychiatrist was able to help her to recognize her angry reaction to the punishment as normal for a child of that age and to see, also, that the father's death soon afterward was coincidental. The exposure of the memory, and the explanation of the effect that it had had on her, served to release her from the phobia to the extent that she was able to return to her job with no further difficulty.

The Parts of the Personality

Id, Ego and Superego

Returning now to the parts of the personality, let us examine the id, the ego and the superego. As the aide will see, it is important to know the levels of the mind first, since these parts of the personality "live" in the mind, so to speak.

The *id*, Freud's term for all instinctive and self-preservative tendencies, sometimes is called the "true unconscious." The id is *what we want to do;* it is purely pleasure-seeking. A newborn baby is, essentially, *all* id, and his wants, which are often primitive, are uncontrolled. If he is hungry, he will make sucking motions and noises; or if he is not fed and becomes frustrated enough, he will scream and kick and clench his fists. If he has the desire to eliminate waste products, he does so, without making any judgment about where, when or how. If he is angry, he will have an infantile tantrum.

Obviously, the id cannot go long uncontrolled, and at the beginning of the toilet-training period, the baby begins to develop a *superego*, or conscience. Now the child must learn the meaning of "yes" and "no," "do" and "don't." As the superego begins to be refined, it makes judgments as to what is right and what is wrong (according to the culture in which one lives) and it exercises control over the id. The superego is *what we have to do.*

At this point, it should become clear that life is one long battle between the id and the superego. There are many things we want to do which are "socially unacceptable," and most of the time the superego wins out, and we conform. Our innate desire for acceptance supersedes our desires for "forbidden fruit." The exceptions occur, of course, when our defenses are down—notably when under the influence of alcohol or other drugs, and when emotional disturbance or, more serious, mental illness, distorts values.

The end-result of the never-ending battle between the id and the superego is the *ego*. The ego is *the self*, the conscious and permanent subject of all experience, the total person. In a sense the ego monitors both the id and the superego because of its function of self-preservation.

Introduction

All his life he had been like other people in that he had made excuses for his behavior when it was not all it should have been. Also, like other people, he had not been aware of excusing himself, and yet, as he learned about all the little human defenses, he began to catch himself using what the inservice instructor had labeled "Defense Mechanisms."

For example, the other night, when he had been home on a weekend, his wife had asked him to get going on that long-neglected porch-painting job, and he had said: "I'm sure it's going to rain—the weather report says so—and it wouldn't dry." Then, the next day, a brilliant sunshiny one, he had gone fishing.

──────────────────────────────4

The Use of Defense Mechanisms

In the foregoing pages it has been shown that the life of the human being is a constant struggle. This struggle is, essentially, between the inner being of himself and all the things outside of himself which directly and indirectly affect him. Man follows three main lines of action when confronted with a conflict or an uncomfortable situation not solved by ordinary means: he can fight; he can take flight; or he can compromise. Obviously, the first two measures are not the healthiest; the third is, for by compromising he is standing back from the painful situation, taking stock of it and devising an acceptable means of resolving his conflict. In order to reach a compromise, one has to give a little, and giving is growing.

Definition. What causes these frequent conflicts in the life of man? Every person has individual wants which, more often than not, cannot be fulfilled because of the disciplines of culture, social conscience, or religious beliefs. When these two forces meet—the individual want versus one of the disciplines mentioned—the person either gives in to the want and behaves in a socially unacceptable manner or compromises by means of a substitute reaction. Such a substitute reaction is termed a *defense mechanism*. The use of a defense mechanism often takes care of the want *in a socially acceptable manner*. Since everyone uses defense mechanisms at one time or another, and since they are an obvious part of the lives of *both* the mentally healthy and the mentally sick, it is essential that the aide be aware of the more important ones, their names and how they are used.

Types of Defense Mechanisms

Rationalization. A girl wishes to go to a dance but is not invited. As the time draws near, she may be heard to make any one of the following explanations: "I couldn't possibly afford a new gown, anyway, and I've worn out all my others!" or, "It will be a dull dance and there's a movie that night that I've been dying to see!" or, "I'm glad I'm not going. That crowd of fellows can ruin a girl's feet!" A student facing an examination for which he has not studied sufficiently may say: "It won't do any good to study. They never ask questions on *that* book!" or, "It would do me a lot more good to sleep or go to a movie than to study that stuff!" or, "If I study it, it will only confuse me!" What are these two people doing? They are *making excuses for themselves,* and this is known as *rationalization.* All of us have encountered patients who are "too busy" to go to the treatment room for an unpleasant medication or refuse to go to a group therapy session because "Mr. D. and Mr. E. do all the talking." It is easy to see that rationalization can become quite a tool with which patients can manipulate the aide unless the aide is able to observe shrewdly when the patient is in earnest and when he is "making an excuse."

Projection. Putting off onto someone else something that you do not like about yourself is known as *projection.* For example, an aide who frequently works overtime and takes on special time-consuming projects may say, "I don't understand these people who drive themselves all the time. Must have a problem they're escaping from, or maybe they want a promotion fast!" Or an aide may complain bitterly that a certain supervisor "never has liked me," when the truth of the matter is that the aide has never liked the supervisor! The simple statement by a patient that, "These people in here are nuts. I shouldn't be here! If I stay much longer, I'll go crazy like the rest of them!" is a sample of projection. Another patient may say, "That guy is 'queer'—he looks at me funny" when one of his own greatest problems is a strong compulsion toward homosexuality. Often, the use of projection by patients can give the aide important clues as to some of the basic problems which are disturbing them.

Identification is a mechanism frequently utilized by patients. It merely means that a person feels a likeness with another person, and it is similar to imitation. Many times, the problem of one patient who refuses to eat will develop into two or three problems of two or three patients who will not eat. An already quiet patient may become very depressed when assigned to a room with another patient who is very depressed. Examples from everyday life are numerous:—children who identify with a television star like Matt Dillon; teen-age girls who copy the hair style of their favorite actress; men who have "morning sickness" when their wives become pregnant. One important thing for the aide to remember about this particular defense mechanism is that patients often will identify with an aide. Therefore, it is obviously necessary that he set a good example—in appearance, manner and action.

Repression. Most people, at one time or another, hear stories of babies who are deformed in some way "because the mother was frightened by an animal while she was pregnant." This has been largely disproved by fact, but it *is* true that we consciously "forget" very unpleasant incidents and often cannot account for unreasonable fears. The process of forgeting" is known as *repression*. Repression is well illustrated by the man who attempts to call a familiar telephone number and finds that he has forgotten the number completely. For some reason or other, either the number of the person being telephoned recalls for him an unpleasant event, *although he is not aware of it,* and he does not *want* to call the number. Thus, he forgets it completely. It may take him some time to remember the unpleasant event which has caused the temporary memory block he is having. A patient consistently refused to join in a knitting project on her ward and reacted with considerable fear toward knitting needles when they were presented to her. She could not state *why* she was afraid of the needles, and it took a long time to find out that as a very young child she had been badly frightened by an older sister who had delighted in painfully poking her with knitting needles after school or in their room at night.

Suppression. Very similar to repression, *suppression* is the forcible exclusion from the memory of some unpleasant event. However, suppression is one of the few mental mechanisms that is used *consciously.* As a simple illustration, let us say that an instructor and an aide have an argument in front of a class. The instructor, who has allowed himself to become very angry and embarrassed, is upset and says to himself: "I'll just forget the whole thing. It's not that important." It is true that he may forget for awhile, but the very next time he sees the aide with whom he argued, the memory will return in all its detail. Thus, suppression is only temporarily effective, so that with more meaningful traumatic events, repression usually is the mechanism in operation.

Compensation is a fairly common defense used among normal people. Almost everyone knows the physically small man who gains power and then wields it without regard for his fellows. Napoleon and Hitler are two significant examples.

In other words, the small man makes up for his feelings of inferiority by developing other substitute capabilities. Some women who want children of their own and do not marry for one reason or another may take up teaching or nursing. In this way, they work and are in daily contact with "substitute children." *Overcompensation* may lead to mental illness, and we have patients who compensate for a low intellect by being bullies—pushing other patients around and making general nuisances of themselves. A patient with a hysterical (without physical cause) paralysis may be overcompensating for her feelings of being an inferior or unfaithful wife. Perhaps, she needs an escape from the responsibilties of raising a family. Overcompensation can mean going to the opposite of what is expected. A young woman whose mother has always insisted on absolute cleanliness and neatness at home may, when she goes to college, have the messiest room in the dormitory.

Regression. Another defense mechanism is called *regression*. One thinks of regression mostly in terms of patients, but in actuality it is fairly ordinary with those who are supposedly mentally well. In brief, regression is an escape *backward* from the strain and the responsibility of adult life. Children can be comfortable with uncontrolled behavior and are not too strenuously criticized for it. For instance, the small child who has a temper tantrum is forgiven and, as much as possible, understood. The adult who has a temper tantrum is looked upon as a badly behaved person and a poor risk in social situations. The person who cries easily, fluently and frequently is also considered as having a low frustration level and as being emotionally unstable. Children cry many times a day, and it is thought of as quite normal. Frequently, we find our patients in a "state of regression"; that is, they have gone back to childish ways—even infantile ways.

The Use of Defense Mechanisms

Thus, as has been mentioned already, masturbation and smearing are two examples of regression in mental patients. Some patients curl up in a corner or under a bench and remain that way for days at a time, only moving when fed or bathed or toileted. Sometimes, when put to bed they will get out and crawl under the bed, assuming the same curled-up position. This is an advanced stage of regression in which the patient returns to prewalking days as a baby. It is a way of running away from the strains of being an adult and having to meet various daily problems.

Displacement. One more defense mechanism is *displacement*. This is the act of discharging an emotional response on a person or thing not originally causing the response. It is used very commonly and is an unconscious reaction. Several years ago, on the cover of a popular national magazine, a series of four pictures appeared.

In the first, Tom's boss obviously is giving him a bawling out; in the second, Tom is home from work and he is berating his wife because supper is not ready; following this is a scene where the wife is scolding the little boy; and, in the final illustration, the little boy is kicking his dog.

Displacement is particularly important because, unhappily, all too often it is the patient who receives the brunt of our displaced frustration or anger. If the supervisor soundly criticizes the aide for an untidy ward on a very busy morning, the aide may, quite unconsciously, be abrupt, harsh and irritable with patients.

There are other defense mechanisms, but they may not be seen very often by the aide. It is essential to remember, however, that defense mechanisms are not solely the property of mental patients. It is well for us to watch ourselves for our use of them. In this way, and by observing patients closely, we can learn more about defenses and can understand them better. By understanding what a patient *is* doing in order to avoid what he *ought* to be doing, the aide can offer more support to him so that he can face up to things and rebuild his feelings of self-esteem.

Introduction

From the children he learned many things. He saw them fight together, play by themselves, cry, become leaders and have tantrums. He heard their curiosity, watched them with their parents, and he began to understand. He was amazed at the similarities between the children and his patients. The patients fought and cried and became leaders and stayed by themselves; he noticed certain of his colleagues behaved like parents with patients — good parents and bad parents. And patients generally reacted in the same ways. He had progressed to a point where he often had to make decisions about the management of behavior problems on his ward. Often, he was unsure, but he continued to observe and read and discuss. He learned not to "label" patients, but to know each one as a person.

———————————————————5

Your Management of the Kinds of Behavior

The teaching of aides, nurses, and others whose job is the care of the mentally ill has had far too much focus on classification. That is, courses have been designed according to a pattern of specific diseases—their cause, symptoms, treatment and outcome. In some respects this has been very damaging, since it does two things: (1) produces a tendency to lump patients into a specific cubbyhole—with a title—thus losing individuality and variation and (2) leaves out much of the understanding of basic personality needs, so important for aides and their colleagues to know. Since all mental patients differ, and their reactions to illness differ, it is much more important to understand the reasons for a patient's behavior than it is to know whether or not he is "manic," "paranoid," or any of the other titles of classification. Many patients exhibit a number of different symptoms which could fit into any one of the various types of illness and by no means follow a set pattern. Classification should only be used as a guide—a means of communication. One gets a general idea of a behavior pattern from the "titles" or the diagnosis." But general is not enough! It is important that the aide, particularly (since he is the one who has to contend with behavior 24 hours a day), know and understand behavior problems so that he can handle them adequately.

For simplicity, behavior patterns have been grouped under eight general headings in this chapter, but it is absolutely necessary for the aide always to keep in mind that his patients who are mentally ill are unpredictable. No patient will behave in an exact manner in any given situation, and it is for this reason that the aide needs to develop an especially acute awareness of the ways of human beings, including himself!

Overactivity

Overactivity indicates intense activity, usually without direction. It can be verbal or motor or both and is not confined to any one type of patient. In fact, any mental patient can become overactive, depending on the given situation and the patient's reaction to it. When overactivity is mentioned to one who is unfamiliar with the mental hospital, the usual impression is a negative one; that is, the patient is pictured as menacing, angry, homicidal and destructive. This, of course, is not the case, and new aides and other personnel working for the first time in a mental hospital are surprised at the small number of patients whose illness manifests itself in this negative fashion. There are patients who talk, sing and write profusely all day and sometimes all night. There are patients who, if allowed, would make beds, scrub floors and walls, clean toilets and so on indefinitely. There are patients who walk and run and dance and are never still. And there are the few who are angrily overactive and destroy hospital property, pick fights, or attempt to harm themselves or others. One thing is certain, and that is that overactivity of any kind demands and receives attention. It is well to mention here that many aides and nurses fall into the trap of giving *most* of their attention to the overactive patients on their ward, leaving quiet, underactive patients to look after themselves.

Overactivity

There are good reasons for this. For one thing, as mentioned above, overactivity demands attention. For another, the overactive patient is usually more "interesting" and often more "amusing" than the quiet one. Still another reason is that it is easier to establish a relationship with an overactive patient, since communication is forthcoming whether it is wanted or not! However, these things do *not* mean that overactive patients need more care. *All* kinds of patients should have as much care as can possibly be given.

Your Management of the Kinds of Behavior

One can always find a stimulus for overactivity, although many times the reasons are subtle and hard to locate. The stimulus may be a very realistic one, such as the visit of a disliked relative, or the annoying noises of a high wind. It may also be emotional as, for instance, the intense guilt feeling of the person who is driven to scrub and sweep and clean all day. Patients can be agitated into disturbance by other patients, or they may see another patient upset, or they may be threatened by a treatment which has not been adequately explained to them, if at all. Frequently, disturbed behavior is the result of fear or loneliness, or both. If one examines the situation thoughtfully one seldom finds anger as the real basis for aggressive behavior; many times it may seem that way because anger will be the initial mask assumed by the patient, and he may shout and walk up and down and become troublesome to all concerned.

What can be done about the overactive patient? He disturbs other patients, upsets ward routines, often frightens personnel, is a problem to himself in terms of his physical well-being, may be destructive of his own and others' property, and is generally considered as a management problem by those caring for him. There are no set rules for handling disturbed patients. There is no one-two-three routine, no particular number of personnel who should be involved, no special "holds" that can be used. People will try to teach this, but in the actual situation it does not work because all kinds of things are involved. For example, the size of the patient, his age, the degree of emotional disturbance, the reason for the behavior, the attitude of the aides, whether or not his doctor is present, whether or not the patient is under the influence of drugs or alcohol, and so on.

Each situation demands its own special handling, and every one will differ. However, there are a few very important generalities that will apply. First of all, disturbed behavior on the part of patients does not need to occur nearly as often as it does. In other words, when the aide *knows* his patient well, he senses when a blow-up is coming, often knows *why* and can take steps to prevent it. An aide has told the following story to illustrate this point:

"We always knew when Mrs. B. was 'going high.' She would take everything in sight and stuff it in the sink and start washing it. Then, we knew we should spend more time and energy with her, letting her talk things out, asking her to help us with our more strenuous routines, such as washing down the porches, and soon she would quiet down."

Another aide tells of a patient who used to ask to be put in seclusion when she herself felt that she was becoming upset. Wisely, they would get a doctor's order, place her in seclusion, and for one or two hours she would bang around and yell out the windows. New personnel who did not comply with her request usually were sorry and ended up having to put her into seclusion by physical force.

Not all signs of oncoming disturbed behavior are this obvious. It takes awhile for the aide to get to know and understand his patients, as it takes time to form any friendship. Thus, an outburst can occur without warning, and the problem becomes immediate and urgent and in need of solution. Here, a second general principle can be utilized. A calm, quiet manner can do more to help the patient than all the orders or force in the world. Such an attitude is futile only when a patient has completely lost control, *which very seldom happens*. Not long ago, a patient was brought into the nurse's office by four aides. She had cut her wrist severely while smashing out a window, and she was covered with blood, angry, frightened, and hurt. A nurse who knew the patient well asked the aides to stand away from the patient, seated her and, lighting a cigarette, gave it to her, saying, "Mary, let's see that thing. Your getting blood all over my office."

The patient quieted down almost immediately and allowed the nurse to examine the cut. The nurse knew Mary well, knew that she hated force, loved cigarettes and possessed enough sense of responsibility to be concerned about messing up the office. Later, Mary walked to the next building with the same nurse, quietly allowed the doctor to suture her cut and returned to her building worrying only whether or not she had missed her supper.

This example brings in a third general principle applicable when patients are overactive, and that is diversion. By offering the cigarette, something Mary was always wanting, and by calling attention to what was happening to the office, the patient was diverted from her initial anger and from the presence of the four aides in the background. She was also *offered* some responsibility in the situation, indicating a certain amount of trust on the part of the nurse.

To illustrate this further, another incident comes to mind. A fairly new patient was busily trying to kick down the door to the ward. She had attracted much attention and was surrounded by all kinds of personnel and numerous patients. Finally, one of the nurses said to her: "Stop kicking that door. We *need* it!" The patient stopped abruptly, laughed and walked away. She later told the nurse that the realization that she was attempting to destroy property belonging to someone else was contrary to her personal principles and when brought to her attention she felt sorry about it and stopped.

Diversion for overactive patients can be more specific. Open-air activity, when the weather permits, allows patients to work off much excess energy that might otherwise be spent in a problematical manner. Walks, softball, volleyball, dancing and ping-pong are simple activities and available in almost any situation. Helping with ward work—bed making, sorting linen, mopping floors, or washing windows—is also an energy-ridding activity. Sometimes, patients who write at great length can be interested in making posters, composing song lyrics, or copying magazine articles. Incidentally, one can get many clues to the reasons underlying overactive behavior by reading some of the material that these busy, writing patients produce!

The fourth and final general principle to remember in the management of overactive patients is that someone should stay with them as much as possible. Among other observations, it is extremely important to note the physical appearance of the patient, for overactive patients frequently develop physical conditions which need attention. If there is evidence of fever—flushing, rapid pulse, bright eyes—this should be brought to the attention of the person in charge. Sometimes, overactive patients neglect to eat and drink enough fluids, and they become dehydrated or develop faulty elimination. The skin may break down—usually first characterized by redness and swelling. All of these things are as much the aide's responsibility as is the patient's emotional comfort.

One final comment on the management of disturbed or overactive behavior has to do with restraint. Recently, an aide remarked that he had read a book not even 100 pages long in which almost 50 per cent of the material was concerned with the "proper" use of mechanical restraints!

For the purpose of this text, the author wishes to state the carefully considered opinion that the use of mechanical restraint is never "proper" or acceptable and demonstrates only a lack of knowledge of something better to do. Mechanical restraint only increases management problems, because, no matter how well administered or how well supervised, *it can do no more than increase fear, tension, anger, suspicion and frustration in an already disordered mind.* Thus, the specific use of mechanical restraint will not be discussed in this chapter dealing with behavior problems. Since, practically speaking, mechanical restraint is still used in some mental hospitals, the aide who is expected to administer it in his particular situation is advised to review other texts in order to ascertain certain general principles regarding restraint. (This discussion does not include medical restraint such as drugs or tranquilizers.)

Underactivity

In many instances, the underactive patient presents a much more serious problem to the aide than does the overactive patient. These are the ones who seemingly do not want attention, who, at any rate, do not make their wants known, whose whole world has slowed up. They are depressed, feel unwanted, lonely, often suicidal and are filled with a mental anguish so great that it seems to be impenetrable both to themselves and to those caring for them. These are the ones who sit or lie all day, and through the night, and apparently live in a world of nothingness. Actually, much seethes in their minds, and their needs are many and great. Besides the things that these patient want, there are things that they do not want. But the uncontrollable listlessness makes it impossible for them to makes these things known. A patient recently said:

"I used to think that if I were ever depressed the one thing that would snap me out of it would be music. Happy music, lots of it, and loud. When it happened to me, when I felt there was nothing to live for, and I had no hope, music was the last thing I wanted. It irritated me and I used to want to smash the ward radio to bits when someone turned it on."

There are really three general types of underactivity. First, there is the patient who cooperates with routine, at a minimum to be sure, but eats and sleeps and bathes regularly. Otherwise, he wishes to be left alone; he does not want to participate in activities and does not converse with either personnel or other patients. Secondly, there is the patient who is profoundly depressed, who does not wish to eat, bathe, shave, talk or even move. Sometimes, these patients become *negativistic;* that is, they balk at every activity, actually refusing to cooperate on any score and sometimes even doing the opposite of what is asked. They often sit, day after day, staring into space, or lie curled up in bed, or on the floor, sometimes assuming weird, uncomfortable postures for hours at a time. Thirdly, we must mention the bed patient who, because of physical incapacity, is forced to take on an underactive role, although not always by choice.

What problems arise for the aide with the underactive patient? Physical breakdown becomes most important because it is visibly foremost. Careful observation and recording must be made of the amount of food and liquid intake, the amount of sleep, the regularity or irregularity of elimination and the condition of the patient's skin. If the aide constantly keeps in mind the fact that all normal human processes are considerably slowed down with this kind of behavior, he realizes the serious consequences that may follow. Patients may become

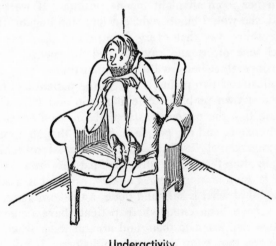

Underactivity

seriously undernourished and dehydrated, thus lowering their resistance and becoming easy prey for infectious illnesses. The problems of feeding such patients and what to do about them will be discussed in Chapter 9. Every effort should be expended to help these patients to eat. Emotional fatigue is not conducive to sleep and, in fact, may foster wakefulness. The patient who expends little, if any, energy is likely to lie awake hours on end at night, and it is important that the aide make *sure* whether or not his patient is asleep. A still form in a still bed does not mean that all is well. A patient sleeping normally breathes differently and usually will stir a little when approached by a person with a light. Patients who are depressed will often retain the products of elimination and should be encouraged to go to the toilet regularly. Severe obstruction has resulted in patients who were neglected in regard to elimination—some even requiring operation. An aide tells the following: "I once had a patient who was almost completely negativistic and mute. She never talked, and often would stand in her room all night in one position. If we put her into bed, she would climb right out and stand again. But the amazing thing was that every four or five days she would approach one of us and say, 'I need an enema.' And she would cooperate wholly with its administration."

This illustrates two points: (1) that the patient had to keep track of her own problems of elimination and (2), which is important, that the patient was actually in good contact with her environment and the people in it, even though apparently noncommunicative! It is absolutely essential to remember that, more often than not, underactive patients are fully aware of what goes on around them. For this reason, it is wise to be very careful of what is said and done in their presence. Many instances have been cited where patients have remembered things that happened to them and around them when, to all appearances, they were completely oblivious.

Skin care requires, for the most part, activity and stimulation of the affected parts. The legs are affected most frequently or, with bed patients, the shoulder blades and the lower back. For the latter frequent alcohol rubs, even though of short duration, and the application of soft powder can do much to prevent the development of the much more difficult problem of bedsores. Bed patients should be turned frequently, kept dry and clean and should have their bed linen tightened and straightened often.

For the patient who is out of bed but severely underactive, short walks (even up and down the ward corridor), simple, rhythmic dance steps, and rest with legs and feet elevated help to eliminate ulcers. Once a patient has been allowed to contract a circulatory ulcer of the lower leg, it is very difficult to rid him of it. If he remains underactive, even though it may heal periodically, it will break down again. If there is time, each underactive patient should have his legs massaged with alcohol once or twice a day.

These things are sometimes difficult to accomplish, because underactive patients do not want to move; they resent being pushed into activity and may even become quite hostile if the personnel are insistent. Even though it may well be understood that the patient wants only to be left alone, it is still important to push some activity. Why do patients become withdrawn and antisocial? How can the aide help them to return to socialization? Many patients withdraw in self-pity. Somehow or other they feel that they have failed deeply and have been rejected by those whom they hold most dear; they have frequent crying spells. It is difficult with this kind of severe grief reaction to convince a patient, more by action than words, that people do like him, want him and desire to be with him. It is a slow, painstaking process, requiring genuine liking for and interest in the patient, as well as faith in his ability to pull himself up by the boot-straps, so to speak.

Other patients may feel extremely guilty about some past happening, imaginary or otherwise, and will constantly berate themselves, particularly in their own minds. This is a deeper problem in which the psychiatrist can do most for the patient, but the aide is responsible for withholding his own judgment and moralization and not inflicting his opinion on his patients. He displays respect for and thoughtfulness about his patient, not allowing himself to increase the patient's guilt intentionally. Still other patients cannot readily account for their feelings of depression and need a willing, listening ear. Often, they are trying to work through the reasons for their feelings of listlessness and apathy and want to talk to someone in the hope that they might discover the roots of the problem.

In the last analysis, one more suggestion is made which applies to both overactive and underactive patients, in fact, to *any* patient. Sometimes, it is very wise to avoid forcing the issue when a sensible number of attempts have been made. Usually, in due time, a patient will cooperate and do what is asked of him, but there are times, as with all of us, when he has to be "in the mood." For example, a young nurse, inexperienced in dealing with mental patients, kept insisting that a patient have her shower along with the rest of her ward group. The patient kept insisting that she was Queen Cleopatra and did not want a bath. The more the nurse persisted, the angrier the patient became. Finally, she turned on the nurse and gave her a scary but not injurious mauling. An aide who had been with the patient a long time later told the nurse that if she had made known, once, what was wanted, the patient, taking her own time, would soon have wandered into the shower room and accomplished the task at hand without assistance.

Thus, routine should not become all-powerful. There is a tendency, at times, for supervisors and other responsible personnel to put order and cleanliness above the personal needs of the patient. Although order and cleanliness are an important aspect of mental health, there are times when they can be postponed in favor of activities for patients which contribute to their emotional well-being. Who has not had the experience of visiting wards where the corridors shine, the dormitories with neatly made beds are locked, chairs and benches are lined up severely against the walls—and the patients? The patients sit idly in chairs, often afraid to move, or are so disturbed that they are somewhere on a back hall in seclusion. Not even a card table and extra chairs are allowed, since they might scratch the waxed floors! A comfortably disorderly ward may not impress important visitors but one finds happier patients there.

Regression

Previous mention of the regressed patient has indicated that the behavior in regression is akin to a moving backward along the scale of growing. Many things about childhood are both pleasurable and comfortable, mainly because social controls do not need to be exerted. Regressed behavior can be a most troubling problem, because it involves feelings of disgust and impatience on the part of the aide. These feelings of disgust and impatience can become so crippling that aides often cannot or will not work on certain "untidy" wards. Very sick patients will urinate on the floor, soil themselves, smear the products of elimination, eat with their hands, become overly affectionate and are not at all interested in the usual, normal activities of the ward. A patient may masturbate openly and excessively or may indulge in overt homosexual relationships with other patients. All of these things are not only disturbing to personnel but also to other patients living in the same ward.

Why do patients revert to this type of behavior when they are very ill? As children they experienced certain pleasurable sensations connected with eating, elimination and sexual activity. They also became aware that certain things they did either pleased or displeased their parents, and that they could "use" their behavior to obtain some of their wants. In some ways, mental illness can be looked upon as an escape. When problems and conflicts become too much for an individual to cope with, he must run away from them. Some people become alcoholic (this, in itself, is a sickness); others may indulge in excessive dissipation, running from one party or night club to another, being sexually promiscuous, or even becoming petty criminals; still others develop all kinds of

Regression

physical symptoms which keep them traveling from one doctor to another, and in and out of various hospitals. The mental patient escapes because he behaves in such an unacceptable manner that he cannot exist outside of the hospital in the community, and he achieves a certain amount of safety and security in the mental hopital where his behavior is accepted and presumably understood. Patients often seem to be engrossed in a world of their own. They take little or no interest in what goes on about them and seem to be perfectly content with their inner world—their thoughts and fantasies and dreams. They seem to lose all social awareness and any good habits that they might have known. They appear to dislike people and will behave as if they want to have nothing to do with others. However, this attitude on the part of patients can be very misleading. Actually, the psychotic patient wants, more than anything in the world to be close to someone—anyone who will befriend him, be patient with him, understand him and be someone whom he can trust. One of the reasons he is sick is because he does not know *how* to get close to anyone, and he has no faith that anyone else knows how. Thus, it will take weeks and weeks, and even months, and possibly years for the person interested in him to prove his trustworthiness to the patient.

This is an extremely difficult thing to do with the regressed patient, because the regressed patient will not take responsibility for himself. If not constantly supervised and directed, he would not eat, would be very untidy, and would sit or stand all day doing nothing.

As we understand the needs of children and the necessity for our tolerant and enduring care of them, so can we understand the regressed patient. He soils himself not because he is a "terrible person" or "just to make work for us" but because he cannot remember to go to the toilet, or he just does not think of it. He seems to have "unlearned" all of the things he once did almost without thinking. The deeper solution to this problem of soiling is, of course, to treat his psychosis. But even more basic is the important part that the aide can play in this treatment. Toilet-training must now start all over. The patient has to be taken to the toilet, even as often as every two hours, and told what is expected of him; he must be encouraged to do his part. An aide tells of her discouragement over such a project:

"I took her religiously to the toilet every two hours for two solid weeks. It seemed almost as if she held everything up until I was to go off duty. Always after our last trip to the bathroom, I would return her to the day room, and everything would come! She never went during a regular trip. I don't think it can be done."

No. It would not be done in two weeks' time. But with endurance and patience, with all aides on the three shifts of duty cooperating, this patient might, after a long time, learn once again to care for her own needs for elimination. It is just possible that in this particular case the aide would quite naturally show her irritation and discouragement to the patient each time she had to clean up after her. The patient might remember that this was a way she had had of "getting even" with her mother when, as a child, she had not obtained something that she wanted. She could well be using the same "weapon" against the aide. It is difficult to be tolerant and even cheerful about such matters, but to be so often makes the task time much shorter.

As children and regressed patients have to be toilet-trained, so they have to be taught how to feed themselves and use the proper utensils. Right here it should be said that in areas where only the "very best" patients are allowed knives and forks, this is practically a hopeless task. An aide tells of an "unofficial" experiment conducted in one of the hospitals in which he had worked:

"The doctor in charge of the men's chronic disturbed unit decided that the use of knives and forks in the dining rooms would involve a minimum of accident as compared with a maximum of benefit to the patient. There were four wards of about 60 patients each—pretty sick guys—and he ordered that all but those in seclusion should be allowed to use knives and forks. It was really wonderful. Guys that had been the most untidy eaters you ever saw suddenly developed good table manners. There seemed to be more conversation at meals. In a year's time we had two injuries. One patient punctured the back of another one's hand with a fork, and one guy gave his throat a superficial cut with a fork. We kept track of the silver. Before each patient left the dining room his place had to show one knife, one spoon, and one fork."

Anyone who can resist eating with his hands when he is faced with, for instance, a pork chop, baked potato and large leaves of slippery, cooked cabbage and only a spoon with which to eat it would have to have infinite patience! And this is a fairly typical hospital meal. Thus, it is little wonder that many patients who have been sick a long time simply eat with their hands because it is easier.

In order to help a patient to redevelop good eating habits, sometimes it is necessary in the beginning to feed him entire meals, sitting with him and talking to him. It is well to encourage him to use his fork whenever he indicates that he wants to and can do so with control. Someday, there will be enough help in the dietary and nursing departments of our large mental hospitals to make it possible for patients to take their time eating; to have meals at more normal hours than 6:30 A.M., 11:00 A.M. and 4:30 P.M.; and for aides and nurses to sit with groups of patients and encourage good eating habits, rather than standing in the doorways making sure that patients eat anything at all and do not carry half the dining room back to the ward with them.

Sexual Problems

In Chapter 3, homosexuality and masturbation were mentioned as something to be expected *during certain stages* of development. However, after these stages of development have passed and these two elements of behavior still persist, it is an indication of serious maladjustment. Patients who have been hospitalized a long time and have little or no outlet for sexual energy may present problems to the aide which are problems of regressed behavior. Patients who engage in overt (open) homosexual activity present a problem to the aide *if* he critically judges rather than tries to understand. There are many reasons why homosexuality exists among hospitalized mental patients. For one thing, the mentally ill person is extremely lonely; he is looking anywhere for the love he never has received; for another, many times, he is not allowed any contact with the opposite sex; for still another, he may never have successfully passed through the latent period of development (where homosexuality is the normal pattern) and has been unable to form any productive relationship with the opposite sex. To express revulsion, verbally or otherwise, does not solve the problem but only increases it. Understanding and tolerance, coupled with the very practical solutions of diverting patients into group activities, separating patients who seem overly attached to one another, and making sure that the patient's doctor is aware of this behavior can usually stop the practice without unduly hurting the patient.

The same principles apply to the patient who masturbates openly and often. This can be extremely disturbing to other patients, and every effort should be made to help the patient to overcome the behavior difficulty. Something else to remember about masturbation is that there may be some very practical reasons for such activity on the part of the patient. Possibly his clothing is too tight; perhaps he has some urinary difficulty and needs a complete physical checkup; possibly he even has pubic lice, a condition which can and should be corrected, immediately. The aide should remember, always, that homosexuality and masturbation are not sicknesses themselves, or the cause of sickness; but they are indicative of sickness and should be regarded as important symptoms. At no time should the aide be critical of or amused at such behavior. It is well to remember always, *it is easier to criticize than to try to understand.*

Addiction

The previous four headings—overactivity, underactivity, regression and sexual problems—cover, very generally, the most common, problematical behavior seen in the mental hospital, particularly in *psychotic* patients.

Addiction requires special discussion (as do neuroses and maladjusted personality patterns which follow), because the manifest behavior of patients suffering from these particular ills is comparatively *normal.* Strictly defined, addiction means *complete dependence on a drug or alcohol* wherein the affected person will go to any lengths to obtain the desired object. Actually, one can become addicted to many things which we write off as "habit"—cigarettes, food, sweets, even people! Certainly, when one persistently pursues something (or someone) that is harmful to oneself, one can legitimately be called "addicted." Chapter 6 will deal with drug abuse.

Alcoholism

Since addicts often use both alcohol and drugs in the process of their illness, the hospitalized alcoholic and addict present some of the same behavioral problems to the aide.

Entire books and dozens of articles are devoted to alcoholism; yet little is really known about its basis. There are estimated to be about 6,500,000 alcoholics in this country (5 per cent of whom would be labeled "severe alcoholics"), and this number grows phenomenally every year. Although much money, research, and study have gone into the problem, most questions about the cause of alcoholism remain basically unanswered. Some believe that certain people have a *tendency* to alcoholism and eventually will become alcoholics no matter how favorably their life may proceed; others believe that it is an acquired illness, brought on by unbearable stress and strain. Most alcoholics will state that it is a physiologic problem—that they have an actual physical craving for alcohol. Probably because of the lack of knowledge about the cause of alcoholism, there is, as yet, no known cure. Alcoholism can only be *controlled;* it cannot be cured.

What the Patient Is Like. Addicts, and this includes alcoholics, basically are lonely people who feel (and often are) rejected by society and by those to whom they are closest. As he becomes more experienced, the psychiatric aide will undoubtedly sense mixed feelings about this group of patients. On the one hand, they are pathetic; on the other, they can be very troublesome while under the influence of alcohol. They can be discouraging, too, because time and time again they avow that they are "cured"; and time and time again they return to the hospital in worse condition than when they left.

In general, alcoholics are above average in intelligence, warm and charming, cooperative and willing and usually very helpful on the ward—once the effects of drinking have worn off. Occasionally, the opposite may be true, and the patient may be sullen, even hostile, and he may be very uncooperative.

Attitude. Certain fundamental attitudes can be assumed by the aide which will be helpful.

NONJUDGMENTAL. Alcoholics Anonymous has a motto which reads: "There, but for the grace of God . . . . (go I)" meaning, of course, that such addiction can happen to anyone. It would appear to be true, too, since known alcoholics come from all walks of life, are of all ages and both sexes. Whatever the personal feeling of the aide toward addiction, he must remember that he is there to help that patient, not to censure him.

HEIGHTENED AWARENESS. The alcoholic is clever and will go to any length to acquire alcohol. Therefore, it is essential to be always alert to the whereabouts of the patient and to his condition. For example, a patient who usually was sullen and defiant always seemed to be more relaxed and cheerful after his wife had visited him. The aides thought that the wife's visits were good for him until one day she was observed sneaking him a pint of gin!

Because alcoholics usually have good superficial insight and can talk intelligently and at length about their problem, it is easy to be drawn into a nontherapeutic web of sympathy and favoritism. One can listen attentively and politely without becoming absorbed in the patient's personal life.

MODERATION. In line with the last paragraph, it is also easy to take advantage of the patient's good will and work potential. One alcoholic patient in an admission ward was very good at accomplishing necessary ministration with acutely ill psychotics. She seemed to have a knack for getting them to eat, to dress, to go to bed, and so on. The aides began to give more and more responsibility to the alcoholic patient until, before too long, both the aides and the patient began to think of the patient as a staff member! This can be a dangerous situation for the patient, the staff, and other patients.

CONCERN FOR PHYSICAL WELL-BEING. Most people know that one of the primary problems of acute alcoholism is the very poor physical condition of the patient, due to his tendency to ignore adequate nutrition and personal hygiene for long periods of time. Often, these patients are admitted in dreadful condition—filthy, dehydrated, constipated, thin and with all sorts of vitamin deficiencies. It is the responsibility of the aide to make every effort to correct all these conditions as soon as possible. Patients on the verge of, or already in, "D. T.'s" (delirium tremens) need constant attention and the reassuring presence of another, stable human being. The hallucinations which this part of the illness produces are horrible, and patients often are literally frightened out of their wits. A patient in severe "D. T.'s" may be in danger of dying, and every medical and psychological aid should be employed to help him.

The Neurotic Patient

Primarily, a neurotic can be defined as a person who has not, through the use of defense mechanisms, been able to make a healthy compromise with his conflicts and whose resulting anxiety must be converted into physical complaints or compulsive, ritualistic behavior. Unlike the psychotic, he does not escape into a world of unreality.

Until recent years, comparatively few patients suffering from neuroses came to the mental hospital. This was because most neuroses do not completely incapacitate people (except in advanced stages), and also because most patients with neurotic complaints could be treated on an outpatient basis. However, with the increased knowledge that early and intensive treatment of emotional ills accomplishes much in the prevention of more serious disorders, more and more patients with a diagnosis of a neurosis are entering hospitals for treatment, many of them on a voluntary (rather than committed) basis.

Numerous nurses and aides who have worked with the mentally ill for a long time feel that there are few patients who are more frustrating and difficult to work with than the neurotic. His illness is usually deep-seated and has served as a "crutch" for many years, so that it is doubly difficult to convince him that there is a "better way of life."

(The aide is referred to Appendix B, under Classification of Mental Illness, for a specific listing of the various neuroses. For the purposes of this discussion, only general comments will be made in relation to the care of the neurotic patient.)

Like the alcoholic, the neurotic patient "looks" essentially normal and he behaves well, too, for the most part. There are exceptions—the compulsive patient who must turn completely around nine times before going through any door; the hypochondriac who constantly harasses personnel for "pills"; the hysteric who is functionally paralyzed and must be given complete nursing care.

In general, the neurotic is presentable-looking, takes care of his own personal needs, joins in ward activities without much prodding and is relatively easy to talk with or persuade to be a fourth at bridge. The outward manifestations of the illness revolve mostly around tension, evidenced by pacing, increased perspiration, lack of appetite and inability to sleep. Probably, the three greatest problems with which the aide has to cope are: (1) the "pill problem"—these patients either want pills all the time, refuse to take them, or they hoard pills for purposes of suicide; (2) the repetitive complaints to which the aide must listen patiently, day in and day out; and (3) the patient's *apparent* inability to help himself, for which only the development of a profound *patience* can be a panacea for the aide.

Sociopathic Personality Disturbances

Of all the distorted personality patterns known to psychiatry, the most baffling is that known as *antisocial reaction*. These patients used to be called "Psychopaths" but now are said to have "Sociopathic Personality Disturbances." If a wise and experienced aide or nurse were asked: "What type of patient in a mental hospital do you consider to be the most dangerous?" in all probability the answer would be, "the Sociopath."

This would not be meant to imply "dangerous" in the ordinary sense, i.e., assaultive, destructive, homicidal, but in the less ordinary sense of the unique *seductiveness* of this kind of patient. They are what someone has termed "morally seductive"; that is to say they are not seductive in the usual sense of the word (sexual) but seductive in their ability to wrap people around their little fingers, so to speak. Because of their tendencies to ignore conformity of any sort and to lead others out of order with them, they can be labeled "dangerous."

As with so many other emotional ills, we are baffled as to the cause of an *antisocial reaction*. Theories include the usual: tendency toward, inherited, poor environmental background, emotional starvation, physiologic. None has been proved conclusively and probably some or all of the "causes" contribute jointly to the reaction. The illness seems to reach its fruition in the late teens and early twenties, for this is the time when the patient usually runs into serious trouble with the law. What to do with these people is a potent sociomedical question. Prisons do not solve the problem; neither does hospitalization. Medication and therapy seem to have little value. In fact, most psychiatrists shy away from attempting to treat a known sociopath, mainly because such people seem to be incapable of forming any significant relationships with others and do not seem to possess any motivation to change.

On the ward they are pleasant, intelligent (usually), interesting, cooperative and so normal-appearing that they present a real problem to instructors with young nursing students or new aides. They lie without a qualm of conscience, coerce other patients into mischief and have moody spells when "crossed" which may erupt in violent anger, destructiveness, and injury. Because they have no conscience, they will glibly apologize, beg forgiveness and promise not to misbehave again, all of which virtually means nothing.

No other illness will test the aide's intelligence, patience and moral self-defense as mightily as this one. However, there are a few suggestions in regard to the management of these patients, which can be utilized without difficulty if the total picture of the illness is grasped with clarity.

Inform the Patient. Most mental hospital wards have routines and rules which are (hopefully) set up for the benefit of the patient group as a whole. These routines have to do with meals, baths, medications, ward housekeeping, clothing and all the other minutiae of daily living. It is most important that the patient with antisocial reaction be fully informed and frequently reminded of these regulations. If he is told the rules clearly, he cannot use his ignorance of them as an excuse.

Be Consistent and Firm. In line with informing the patient, the aide must be *consistent* and must be *firm* in his enforcement of the rules. It is always unwise to give in, even once, because this type of patient will take full advantage of any let-down of the bars. In other words, no exceptions should be made under ordinary circumstances.

Maintain Reserve. Many tragic happenings have resulted when a staff member has allowed himself to be taken in by the sociopath's appearance of normality. One such instance occurred some years ago in the Midwest. A nursing student had been working with an attractive young man who had been admitted for observation after a series of arrests for offenses ranging from "misdemeanor" to "driving so as to endanger life." The instructor had left word with the charge aide that the student was never to go anywhere alone with this patient, a ruling of which the student was also aware. One day, in the absence of the charge aide, the student was given permission by the supervisor to accompany the patient through the hospital tunnel to occupational therapy. She was found a short time later, sexually assaulted and murdered.

Although this is perhaps an extreme case in point, there is

no doubt that the greatest hurt the sociopath can do lies in his lack of concern for those who allow themselves to become emotionally involved with him. This happens all too frequently in the world outside the hospital. The aide should train himself to maintain a friendly reserve in his relationships with the sociopath.

Limit Trust. It is difficult not to trust a patient whose behavior has been exemplary for an extended period of time. However, it appears that this is precisely the "out" the sociopath watches for. He is friendly, well-behaved, helpful and cooperative and does not ask any special favors. Someone on the staff may decide that he can be trusted to work outside on the hospital grounds and this is when he will take the first opportunity to walk off and, inevitably, cause more trouble for his wife or family or guardian.

Keep the Patient Busy. A child, more often than not, gets into mischief when he is idle and finds time hanging heavily on his hands. So it is with the sociopath. It is during such periods that he plots, with another patient or two, to overcome the night aide, get his keys and leave the hospital. Or he may spend his time persuading "privileged patients" to bring him matches so that he can set a fire. This type of illness is best managed on the ward by fairly continuous activity—either work or recreation. For younger patients, a school program to enable them to finish high school may be very therapeutic.

Mental Retardation

Although it is true that some psychiatric aides will not have to care for the mentally retarded, most of them will, for practically all psychiatric facilities have some mentally retarded patients *who are also psychotic* or, at least, severely disturbed emotionally. Also, mental retardation has come in for some important consideration in recent years, and the aide should have an understanding of the problem. Because the mentally retarded display special kinds of behavior, a few suggestions are offered for their care.

Most mentally retarded patients are sent, initially at least, to a psychiatric facility because they have become unmanageable at home or in a school or an institution specializing in the care of this particular type of problem behavior.

Mental retardation, contrary to popular belief, is not primarily due to heredity. The most frequent causes are injury or illness occurring before, during or shortly after birth. For example, we know that childhood measles and its occasional complication, encephalitis, can cause severe emotional and intellectual deterioration. However, researchers have revealed some conclusive relationships between heredity and retardation in the studies on the condition called phenylketonuria. The earlier the diagnosis of PKU, the better the chance of preventing the retardation which results from the disease. A rigidly controlled diet, including a special food product* low in phenylalanine (which persons with PKU are unable to metabolize) but providing sufficient protein for growth and repair, results in marked increase in intellectual capacity. Studies have shown that tests of blood and urine can detect this condition shortly following birth, and that presumably PKU is a *preventable* condition.

The mentally retarded patient, though he may be infant or adult, is *like* a child; he thinks and acts like one. Therefore, he must be treated essentially as a child. He is capable of love, and should be loved; he craves attention, which should be granted within practical limits. Promises to him should not be made unless they can be followed through, for when he is disappointed or "crossed," he has temper tantrums. He cannot be trusted in matters requiring selective judgment, because his judgment is impaired. He delights in childish

---

* Lofenalac®, Mead Johnson

playthings and interests and no more should be expected of him.

In a ward devoted specifically to the mentally retarded, there are childish fights, childish (open) affection and childish "wolfing" of food. In regard to the last, a striking example comes to mind. In a large ward for severely retarded men, the aides had a real problem on their hands whenever frankfurters were served at the noon meal. Some of the patients would try to swallow the frankfurters whole, and the results, of course, were serious. After a number of the patients had nearly strangled, frankfurters were omitted from the dietary list for that ward. Perhaps, it would have been even better if the franks had been cut up before they were served to patients.

Mental retardation is dealt with in terms of the *degree* of retardation. Many so-called "educable" patients make excellent workers—on the ward, in the kitchen, on the grounds, or doing housework in the dormitories and the residences. A surprising number can be prepared vocationally for work in the community and are able to move into foster homes where they help with the farming, household chores, or assist the "head of the house" with carpentering, painting, and so on.

Tolerant and understanding supervision is a most important part of the total care of the mentally retarded. Like children, they need and want supervision. We once had a patient we felt could take care of herself, so we allowed her to come back, alone, through the tunnel from her noontime job in the cafeteria. Unbeknown to us, she encountered male patients on these trips, and we soon had an unsanctioned pregnancy on our hands!

Although mental retardation is a baffling, sometimes depressing, often frustrating problem to the aide, it should be handled by kindness, patience, and an innate desire to develop whatever potential may be there.

Introduction

As he grew older in his job, new areas, of concern to him, opened up. More and more young people (often labeled "hippies") were being admitted and their admitting diagnoses frequently read, "Drug abuse." His neighbor's oldest girl had gotten in trouble with the police for possession of marijuana, and he worried about his own children "experimenting."

Listening to the doctors talk in the office in the mornings, he gathered that, as yet, there was no real cure for "hard" drug users. He asked to visit the hospital's Methadone unit and, after talking to some of the patients there, discovered that they held conflicting opinions about the benefits of the Methadone program.

Drug abuse patients were not hard to care for—after they got over their withdrawal symptoms. Except that is, for the few who had been on an LSD "trip." Observing them was rather frightening.

—6

Drug Abuse

Because drug abuse—particularly among the young—has become a terrifying fact of life for many families and individuals, it needs special discussion. This is particularly true since psychiatric aides and other mental health workers are branching out and working in various facilities in the community.

The drug problem is by no means confined to the urban ghetto areas. Affluent suburbia and staid rural communities are equally in trouble. And trouble it is. The big monster, of course, is heroin. Most physicians, law enforcement officers, addicts and ex-addicts admit that there is no cure—to date—for heroin addiction. Federal authorities estimated in 1959 that there were about 100,000 heroin users in the United States. Today they conservatively state that there are probably 100,000 in New York City alone. Most experts estimate that this figure represents about half of the heroin users in the United States.

The psychiatric aide is bound to encounter the drug problem in all age groups in his daily work, perhaps in his own children, and even, in some instances, in his personal life. For this reason, this chapter will be devoted to the most commonly used drugs, what they do, and what treatment methods, meager though they are, are in use today. Drug addicts do reach the hospital, but the greatest problems are still out in the communities.

Heroin

Because the use of heroin can be fatal, both physically and psychologically, and because the traffic in this drug has grown into a fantastic "big business," it presently demands a large share of the attention of physicians, law enforcement officers, school officials, and families. Heroin was developed as a synthetic derivative of opium in Germany late in the 19th century. At that time it was used as a morphine substitute and "cough suppressant." First reports on addiction to this drug began to appear around 1910. Today it has been called "the most readily available drug on the streets."

A "language" has developed along with the skyrocketing rate of heroin addiction. There are "hustlers," "pushers," "inducers," and "users"—the *hooked*. Users call it "horse," "dope," "junk," "stuff." Heroin is taken by various means: sniffing, injecting the liquefied drug just under the skin and, most dangerous, "mainlining," or injecting it directly into a vein. The last method is dangerous not only because of the risk of overdose, but because the needles that are used are often dirty and can produce hepatitis or tetanus. (In New York City alone, there were 900 heroin-related deaths in 1969, and 224 of those who died were teenagers.) Cost to the addict can run as high as $100 a day. This, of course, leads to stealing, and, worse, assault and even murder.

The effect of heroin is sometimes described as a "high" which lasts for several hours. The "high" is not really high; the addict may be drowsy and has no interest in food, sex, or even companionship. After a time, the heroin addict develops a tolerance for the drug and needs increased amounts of it to satisfy his craving. He knows that if he is cut off from his supply he must endure the agony of withdrawal.

Some treatment has been tried. In Great Britain physicians are allowed to prescribe maintenance doses of heroin to known addicts. This program has not been successful except for the fact that it has cut down illegal trafficking of the drug.

Synanon, founded in 1958, is similar to Alcoholics Anonymous. It has been successful only with those addicts who manage to stay within its control and surveillance. As with Alcoholics Anonymous, the principle in Synanon is that ex-addicts who are "off the stuff" go at still-"hooked" addicts with an encounter group approach that at times can be psychologically brutal. Synanon has had difficulty because the program controls only temporarily; addicts "slip" just as alcoholics "slip."

One of the most effective methods of treatment is that which substitutes methadone, a considerably less expensive, legal drug, for heroin. It is also the program of treatment which the psychiatric aide is most likely to find himself involved in. However, the methadone maintenance programs, begun in 1964, involve more than simply a switch to a considerably less harmful addiction. Besides the administration of doses of methadone, addicts are given group and individual therapy, counseling, and vocational training. Psychologically, the aim is toward *control of self*. Many ex-addicts who have been through the program remain on to help other addicts—again a likeness to Alcoholics Anonymous.

In the psychiatric hospital or psychiatric unit of the general hospital, most heroin addicts, once detoxified, spend many months in an intensive therapeutic regime of rehabilitation.

The aide should familiarize himself with the whole problem of serious drug addiction (heroin addiction) because he needs to be ever watchful for: (1) evidence of withdrawal; (2) evidence that drugs are being obtained—from inside and outside; (3) the addict's need for extra support; and (4) the addict's attempts to "put one over" on him. The aide's role is one of supportive, nonjudgmental participation, and he should have the ability to recognize when his patient may be "slipping." Such things as routine searching or too-close supervision of patients' visitors should be avoided.

LSD

There are a number of psychedelic drugs, but LSD (lysergic acid diethylamide) is best known because of the wide publicity it has received in recent years. It was first developed in 1938, and for some 20 years it was a drug of high research interest. In fact, it was tried as a therapeutic agent for such problems as alcoholism and intractable pain. It has a very significant effect on the mind but very little effect on other physiological function. It achieved it greatest prominence in the late 1960's as a drug favored by "hippie" communities like the one in San Francisco's Haight-Ashbury district. Most psychiatric aides will encounter the victims of LSD either in the emergency room (their condition resembles severe delirium tremens) or when a victim is admitted who apparently has suffered irreversible damage from the use of LSD.

The injection of LSD causes intense psychological and emotional reaction. It can produce vivid and sometimes terrifying hallucinations, extreme changes of mood (either very euphoric or very depressed), and significant defects in concentration, memory, judgment, and sense of time and self.

The aide, into whose care the LSD patient eventually falls, needs especially to give emotional support, and perhaps to provide gentle restraint. Tranquilizers may be ordered. Careful surveillance is a must. Occasionally, a preschizophrenic individual "takes a trip" with LSD and does not come out of it. When this happens he may have to be hospitalized for a long time.

Fortunately the use of LSD seems to be declining rapidly, probably because its serious after-effects have been quite well publicized.

Barbiturates and Amphetamines

Probably the most frequently abused drugs (often without coming to anyone's attention) are the barbiturates—Amytal, Seconal, phenobarbital, Nembutal, and so on. One of the reasons for this abuse is that these drugs are dispensed relatively freely for such common present-day complaints as sleeplessness, headaches, tension, anxiety, "nervous stomach," and a host of others. The cycle of addiction often "creeps up" on the patient when he begins to use barbiturates as crutches which enable him (or so he believes) to face the intolerables of his life more easily. Eventually, however, he becomes physiologically, as well as psychologically, dependent on his "sedative" and it is then that he gets into trouble.

Equally abused are the stimulant drugs, the amphetamines, popularly known as "pep" pills. Dexedrine, Dexamyl, Ritalin and other similar drugs give people a false energy, a zest for living and working which often belies depression. Some people get "hooked" on amphetamines when they use "diet pills," which often contain as much as 15 mg. of dextro-amphetamine.

The treatment is gradual withdrawal, and it must be accompanied by a large measure of careful physical observation, emotional support and tolerance on the part of nursing personnel. Psychotherapy, preferably on an individual basis, often helps the patient recognize the underlying reasons for this dependence on the drug. One other thing that the aide should be aware of is the patient's attempts to hide pills, especially during the early phase of withdrawal, so that careful but unobtrusive surveillance is essential.

Marijuana

To date, so little is known, scientifically, about this drug that it is difficult to say what it does, why it's used, or what can be done to prevent, or at least inhibit, its use. The drug itself, a member of the *Cannabis* family, has been known, and known as a social problem, for hundreds of years. In the United States, the use of marijuana aroused public concern by the 1920's, and by 1930 the Harrison Narcotics Act had imposed severe penalties on not only its users, but the pushers who sell it. In the 1970's, as anyone who reads newspapers and magazines and watches television knows, the problem of "pot" has reached what some experts term epidemic proportions.

One of the reasons for the great concern over the use and abuse of marijuana is its accessibility to and popularity among the young and the very young. From college students, its use has now spread down to high school and junior high school students as "the thing to do." Many middle-aged "intellectuals" —college professors, lawyers, physicians, and so on—have also taken to marijuana for their "kicks."

Even though concentrated doses of marijuana can cause hallucinations, disorientation, and even psychotic episodes, these reactions are rare. Young people, including younger *patients* with more serious hang-ups, ask: "Why shouldn't I smoke 'pot'?" and there are no reliable, statistically backed-up answers. The adolescent has tremendous needs for peer acceptance and he is constantly enduring the struggle of mixed ideologies and philosophies. He reasons: "I see my parents drinking and smoking" (both proved harmful—and the adolescent knows it) "and I can't see the harm in smoking 'pot'."

Until considerably more research is done probably the most substantial argument against the use of marijuana is that it *may* easily lead to experimentation with—and often addiction to—the "harder" drugs. And, even that argument is considered by many experts as a dubious one.

Introduction

Part of the long-term plan for his orientation to the hospital and the wards included spending several weeks in each special therapy unit. He learned that there are specific and obvious ways to help patients, but that the process of healthful relatedness with others was still most important. His major role in the therapies was concerned with the patients' welfare before and after treatments. For the first time, he really saw the need for careful observation of physical signs and symptoms. He learned elementary first aid and found it useful both at work and at home.

Your Role in the Special Therapies

In the agonizing search for an answer to the tremendous problem of mental illness, many treatments have been introduced. Some of these treatments have been valuable and continue to be used today, while others have been cast aside as worthless. Many years ago, it is said, patients were taken out in the dead of winter and plunged into icy water as a form of "shock" therapy! Today, we would look with horror upon such an inhuman procedure. The famous "tranquilizer chair" invented and used by Dr. Benjamin Rush in the early 19th century was another long-since outmoded method of treatment. In early Grecian and Roman temples, music and dancing were provided as therapy for patients and only in recent years are assuming their rightful importance as therapeutic tools.

Because of the many variations in specific procedure routines for special therapies, no attempt will be made here to outline exact duties for aides. Most mental hospitals have their own procedure books, and although there are similarities and in some instances standardizations, an outline in order of steps taken for each form of therapy would be virtually useless. The issue of individual differences in patient behavior and reaction again becomes a focal point. Further, each physician administering special therapies has his own preferences for the kinds of assistance he receives.

Therefore, particular emphasis will be placed on the all-important periods preceding and following treatments. During those times the aide faces his most challenging responsibility for the effectiveness of treatment, and for the ultimate physical and emotional comfort of his patients. Certain logical reminders will be offered, as, for example, the discomfort and the inevitable embarrassment inflicted on the patient who goes for electric shock therapy with a full bladder; but information in regard to the position of the patient, how to hold or restrain him during treatment, or a description of the equipment needed will be left for individual institutional orientation.

It is often said that unless one actually lives an experience one can never fully appreciate all of the factors involved. Thus, it is difficult (unless they themselves have been sick) for aides and other personnel caring for psychiatric patients to evaluate and understand the many feelings with which the patients must cope while undergoing therapy. An awareness must be developed which can detect fear, even through a masterful bluff, or hopelessness, even though optimism is the evident mood.

Group and Individual Therapy

Of all the treatments for the mentally ill which have been "invented," used, discarded and sometimes reused, psychotherapy undoubtedly holds the key to recovery for thousands of emotionally disturbed and sick people. It is perfectly safe to state that all the treatments described in the following pages could be—and are—*more effective when supplemented by psychotherapy*. It is gratifying to note that individual or group psychotherapy in the more "technical" sense (that is, conducted by a person well prepared in the necessary *technics* and understandings) is becoming more available to many people before they ever reach the stage of hospitalization.

In the broadest sense of the word, *psychotherapy can be defined as a supportive, understanding and tolerant process with a patient extended through speech and action by a person supposedly in command of his own behavior.* Viewed in this way, it can safely be said that it has been in process in mental institutions for a long time, even though it is only in recent years that its name has been coined, and its specific use limited to trained personnel. Untold numbers of aides and nurses have been almost solely responsible for the recovery of some patients, and yet one seldom hears about it. Only the patient who has gotten well will occasionally give credit to the aide or the nurse who helped him most.

The following is part of a personal letter from a former patient: "I shall never forget what she did for me. I was finally convinced of her conviction that I would get well. I had a hard time believing that she would come back, day after day, to endure the verbal abuse I gave her. I never knew a person who understood me so well, who didn't give in to me unless she thought it was right for me. I felt that I could tell her anything—which was what I needed most in the world to do."

Such a tribute, coupled with the knowledge that one more person has been rescued from the lengthy pain of mental illness, must make many a difficult work day easier for this particular aide.

During the present period of crippling shortages of professional personnel trained in the various specific schools of psychotherapy, there still exist the masses of patients. Many of the patients never experience formalized psychotherapy. Many never will. Occasionally, somewhere in the "back wards" an aide or a nurse takes a special interest in a patient or a group of patients and meets with them two or three times a week. No deep interpretation of the group's conversation takes place, but somehow, once in a while, somebody gets better. Perhaps, the regular group meetings have nothing to do with it. But what else is responsible? It is true that such groups are not psychotherapy groups but assume more of an air of socialization therapy. Psychotic patients, living in the same ward year after year, often do not even know each other's names. They seem to be concerned with no one but themselves. In a socialization group they learn names and associate them with faces; they develop a feeling for one another and are able to show likes and dislikes. The role of the aide in initiating and sustaining such groups, or in working out a therapeutic interpersonal relationship with a single patient, is a subject for debate. Certainly it must have the sanction and the interest of the doctor, and certainly it cannot be done by everyone. But since it exists in certain areas, it is definitely worthy of mention.

The report of the Joint Commission on Mental Illness and Health has given heart-warming impetus to the theory that there are many workers in the psychiatric hospital setting who can utilize psychotherapeutic technics effectively. It recommends as follows:

That nonmedical mental health workers with aptitude, sound training, practical experience and demonstrable competence should be permitted to do general, short-term psychotherapy, namely, treating persons by objective, permissive, nondirective technics of listening to their troubles and helping them resolve these troubles in an individually insightful and socially useful way. Such therapy, combining some elements of psychiatric treatment, client counseling, "someone to tell one's troubles to," and love for one's fellow man, obviously can be carried out in a variety of settings by institutions, groups and individuals, but in all cases should be undertaken under the auspices of recognized mental health agencies.*

More specifically, the aide does have a definite and recognized role in the implementation of group and individual therapies being conducted by professional personnel on his ward. He is depended upon to gather the patients for the meetings and to return them when the meeting is over. He will be asked to contribute information about patients' behavior before and after group therapy or individual therapy. Sometimes he is asked to sit in on the meeting to help observe what goes on, and occasionally he may be asked to record or to write down what transpired during the meetings.

With the increase in the use of group and individual psychotherapy in our large public mental hospitals more and more patients are being helped than ever before. It is important that the aide understand the basic processes of psychotherapy so that he can make careful observations concerning patients who are receiving it. Often, there is a carry-over from the therapeutic session into the ward setting, and information about such behavior can be of utmost importance to the group leader or the individual psychotherapist. Psychotherapy involves taking a long, honest look at oneself; and this can be, and is, at times, a *painful* process. The person (or persons) closest to a patient undergoing psychotherapy needs a reservoir of tolerance and support in order to "stand by" during these painful periods.

The Ataraxic Drugs (Tranquilizers)

In looking back over the general history of mental illness, one is struck by the fact that it has continually baffled physicians and others in the health profession. Countless theories

---

* Action For Mental Health, Final Report of the Joint Commission on Mental Illness and Health, New York, Basic Books Inc., 1961.

have been developed of which all but a few have been discarded. Likewise, countless remedies have been developed, none of which has, as yet, demonstrated any *wide-scale* results. Here, in the late decades of the 20th century, we are still faced with the problems of hundreds of thousands of hospitalized patients and other untold thousands of people outside of hospitals who are suffering from the pain and the discomfort of emotional distress. Many of the remedies which have been introduced have received extravagant publicity and have been optimistically labeled "new cure" or, somewhat more modestly, "new hope" for the mentally ill. One of these is the so-called "tranquilizing drugs." Tranquil means peaceful, quiet, and calm, so that this term is really not quite appropriate for the realistic effects of the drugs. Ataraxia means "a detached serenity," or the ability to face one's responsibilities, conflicts, and problems without undue agitation or loss of control. Observation of hospitalized patients, generally, indicates that the drugs alone do not *cure* patients. Rather, they alleviate the symptoms, the "acting-out," of emotional disorders. They help to make the patient available for therapeutic interpersonal relationships—positive communications. Mental hospital wards today are relatively quiet and pleasant, the patients keep themselves neat and clean, and patients and personnel together engage in constructive group activities. Some aides who worked in mental hospitals 15 or 20 years ago and then left to go into different kinds of work have now returned to work as psychiatric aides. They are amazed at the emphatic change in ward atmosphere which has taken place in the short span of 10 years or so. No longer are wards crowded with noisy, untidy and aggressive or regressive patients. The teaching of psychiatric nursing to nursing students and psychiatric aides has become a new and formidable challenge. Because of the *effect* of the drugs on patient management, teaching must now be concentrated in the all-important combined areas of *communications* and *interpersonal relations* (Chap. 2).

There are a number of important things which the psychiatric aide needs to know about the ataraxic drugs. Because of the still-unsolved problem of the shortage of registered nurses in mental hospitals, it is frequently the aide who gives medications to his patients. Therefore, he should know (1) something of the background, (2) the technics of administration and (3) the effects, both good and bad, physical and emotional, of the various drugs.

There are literally dozens of new ataraxic drugs on the market. Since 1953, the use of the "miracle drugs" in psychiatry has increased by such leaps and bounds that it can be called nothing less than phenomenal. Obviously in this text it is impossible to list all of the drugs, their administration and their side-effects. However, seven of the most commonly used (four tranquilizers and three antidepressants) will be described briefly to give the aide some basis for further study on drug therapy.

Tranquilizers. *Chlorpromazine, U.S.P. (Thorazine)*, was one of the first drugs used in treating the mentally ill, and it is still one of the most popular. It is a synthetic product of the 20th century, developed after careful and controlled scientific research. It is used principally in the alleviation of anxiety, tension, and agitation, and also to lessen motor activity. It is interesting to note that it is used sometimes in general medical conditions such as nausea and vomiting.

It is particularly important for the aide to be aware of the side-effects of chlorpromazine (usually given in dosages of from 10 to 400 milligrams daily). The more common untoward effects are: dryness of mouth, dermatitis (rash), nausea and vomiting, parkinsonism (tremors, rigidity), and occasionally jaundice.

Promazine Hydrochloride, N.F. (Sparine), is similar in use, effects, dosage, and side-effects, except for jaundice, although after having previously taken chlorpromazine, a patient may develop jaundice and/or liver dysfunction on taking promazine.

Reserpine, U.S.P. In contrast with Thorazine's newness, Rauwolfia root (from which reserpine is extracted) has been used in India for hundreds of years as a "tranquilizer." It has a sedative (and antihypertensive) effect and is used principally in the management of patients with anxiety or tension neuroses. Although it has a low toxicity, many side-effects may follow large doses—among them are nasal stuffiness, diarrhea, insomnia, nervousness, weakness, fatigue, muscular aching, nightmares and suicidal tendency. The usual dosage is from 0.05 to 10 milligrams daily, and action is often slow; effects may not be seen for several weeks.

Meprobamate, N.F. (Equanil, Miltown). This drug has very low toxicity and therefore is commonly used with outpatients who are experiencing anxiety or tension states. It has been used effectively in treating alcoholism and because it is a skeletal muscle relaxant, is used in the general hospital for burns of the extremities, orthopedic problems, and other conditions requiring mild tranquilization. Given in doses of from 100 to 400 milligrams a day, the mild side-effects would include rashes, itching, occasional chills and fever, and dizziness.

Antidepressants. Because electric shock therapy is not often used now nor is it always effective in depressive states, some of the newer drugs, in combination with psychotherapy, have been very influential.

Amphetamine and dextroamphetamine (Benzedrine and Dexedrine). Used mostly for mild depression of mood, easy fatigability and apathetic reaction, this group is relatively dangerous because addiction may occur. Other toxic symptoms are common and sometimes severe. They may aggravate anxiety, produce insomnia, increase irritability, and intensify overactivity. The patient may show pallor or flushing, have pain in the chest, or faint. These drugs are given in average daily doses of from 5 to 20 milligrams and should not be taken outside of medical supervision. Unfortunately, they are often used indiscriminately along with "diet fads," sometimes with unhappy results.

Methylphenidate (Ritalin) is not used as extensively as it was when first introduced. It has less side-effect than the amphetamines, but it is also less effective. The average dosage is 20 to 30 milligrams a day.

Imipramine (Tofranil). This drug is being used increasingly in place of electric shock therapy. It seems to be particularly beneficial in those depressions where sadness, hopelessness, guilt, personal inadequacies, and loss of ambition occur. Personal observation of patients over the past several years leads to the conclusion that it is especially effective in "middle-age depressions."

The usual dosage is 25 milligrams four times daily, which can be increased to 200 milligrams per day when indicated. Side-effects are usually not severe and include: profuse perspiration, fatigue, insomnia and blurring of vision. Extreme caution must be used with this drug in the treatment of elderly patients and patients with impaired cardiovascular systems.*

The Techniques of Administration. Since each mental hospital develops its own specific techniques for the administration of medications, only two points will be made in relation to the tranquilizers. One, the obvious warning that these drugs, like any others in the mental hospital, always must be actually *taken* in the presence of the aide or the nurse. A patient can

---

* For further information on the drugs mentioned in this section and other drugs, the aide is referred to the pharmacology books listed under Appendix B.

save Thorazine tablets as well as Amytal Sodium, Phenobarbital, or any of the other sedatives. And they can be just as harmful! The other is the inestimable importance of careful observation of the patient who is receiving the drug. For example, a patient's dosage may be too high; he may be extremely lethargic and ashen in coloring—in other words, he may look sick! It is the aide's responsibility to report these symptoms to the nurse or the doctor at the earliest possible moment.

The Effects, Good and Bad. One might correctly say that it is still difficult to prognosticate the effects of the ataraxic drugs. Will the patient's improvement last? (Readmission rates have been very high among the patients discharged within any given year.) Will certain patients returned to the community, or even patients who are "hospital-adjusted," remain "better" *without drugs?* What is the long-term effect of the drugs? *How important a factor is the close, personal contact necessarily involved between nursing personnel and patients as drugs are actually being administered?* These are only a few of the potent questions which need to be studied extensively before we can draw conclusions.

In general, the *good* effects of the drugs are obvious. Our patients are now people with whom we can communicate. They are people about whom we can feel optimistic and hopeful. Although the task of communication becomes a more difficult challenge, our patient-connected tasks become easier (personal hygiene, feeding, housekeeping).

Because the ataraxic drugs have been in use for less than 20 years, much more research and study are necessary before their assets and liabilities can be appraised confidently. But the ever-increasing numbers of patients who have been helped by the drugs are evidence enough of their positive value, both now and in the future.

Electric Shock Therapy

Many people have commented that one of the prominently remembered scenes in the old movie *The Snake Pit* was that which depicted the administration of electric shock therapy. For most it was an alarming rather than a reassuring representation with its black shock box, weird music and the equally weird interplay of blurred faces, forms and lights. To the patient for whom it is prescribed, it becomes a very real and terrifying experience. The aides and the nurses working in electric shock units have long been puzzled as to the reason for this overpowering fear which makes their job

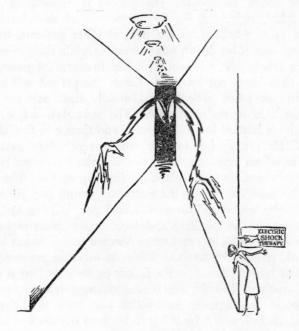

This is the feeling.

so much more difficult. From time to time aides have ventured theories on the subject in ward classes. For one thing, there is the ever-present hangover of patients who have had the treatment, or those who are presently having it and declare open rebellion to the treatment in the presence of new patients. Such expressed fear on the part of fellow-patients can undo the most sincere efforts at reassurance on the part of the aide, even before such efforts are begun. It represents an ongoing lack of communication among patients, doctors, and other personnel as to what an electric shock treatment actually involves. For example, the very busy doctor may inform his patient that tomorrow he will begin a series of electric shock treatments. The patient is immediately and thoroughly frightened, for he has witnessed the aforementioned open rebellion on the part of other patients; consequently, even if his doctor takes time to explain the procedure to him briefly, the information is lost because the patient is more than likely not listening. Later, the patient will make inquiries of other patients, and usually their answers will provide little or no satisfaction. The next day, bright and early, he is hustled to the bathroom, and thence to the "shock room." He usually has to wait with several other patients, some of whom may be actively resisting the treatment. When his turn comes, he is instructed to climb up on the table, and open his mouth to receive the customary mouth gag. He looks up into the impersonal faces of 4 or 5 people (it is unlikely that they will be familiar) and feels several pairs of hands clamp down on his legs and arms. Another pair of hands holds two cold pads on his temples. When he awakens, he struggles to orient himself. Possibly, the fellow in the next bed is tossing, breathing heavily and even making strange sounds. Somebody gets him up and walks him back to the ward where, too frequently, he is left to his own devices and a cup of coffee. For the rest of the day, he readjusts to ward routine, all the while struggling to remember things, and to reassociate himself into the ward group.

The above is *not* typical of all mental hospital shock units and shock routines, but sadly, it does represent the *usual* experience which the patient undergoing E.S.T. must endure. Nobody wants the patient to feel this way, but time-honored reasons continue to exist—shortage of personnel and never enough time to do all that has to be done. Not *all* patients receiving this kind of therapy are so obviously frightened that they become resistive. Some patients go quietly and with some resignation, but when they are able to talk about the experience, they admit an unexplainable dread. Conversations with many patients, investigation of the literature concerning electric shock, and the considered opinion of authorities in the field indicate that *there is no pain associated with the actual treatment.* And yet there is fear, and fear can be extremely painful. No one likes the minor everyday shocks received while opening the car door, or plugging a lamp into the wall socket. The idea of electricity has many fearful associations as in the case of people who run and hide during an electric storm. Thus, the patient may even be afraid that he will die.

Still, a third possible explanation has deeper psychological implications. Basically, electric shock is used to reduce tension, thus making the patient easier to approach psychotherapeutically. One of the common after-effects is a temporary loss of memory. The patient who has severe guilt feelings regarding his fantasy life may wonder what has transpired during the treatment. What has he said? He is much like the person who has had a general anesthetic and asks sheepishly, "How did I act? What did I say?" He is really afraid that he may have said or done something "wrong."

In some hospitals, electric shock therapy is given right on

the ward, although, of course, away from other patients. This system has many advantages, for not only does the patient remain in familiar surroundings, but he is also attended by personnel whom he knows and feels he can trust. He is in his bed and thus does not have to be moved "as soon as possible" to make room for another patient. He can take a shower, dress, and join others in the day hall while he has breakfast. There may be volunteers present who will talk with him, serve him a second cup of coffee, or, if he feels like it, encourage him to join a game of cards.

A patient needs to take a shower and change his clothes after shock. He needs to get the electrode jelly out of his hair, and to brush his teeth. Attempting to regain emotional equilibrium requires the presence of his reassuring friend, the aide. If he is nauseated or has a headache, he should be allowed to lie down for a while. Following lunch, some diversion is needed, such as a walk, a movie, or dancing. Since electric shock is considered to be much more valuable when accompanied by group or individual psychotherapy, this hour is most fruitful when held on the same day as treatment.

An aide tells of an "unofficial" project similar to this which she tried with a small group of patients receiving E.S.T. on her ward. Since she was on the afternoon shift she was not present during or immediately following treatments. However, she heard patients talk to each other about it and sensed their apprehension on the evenings before treatment. She began sitting with them for a while after supper, encouraging them to talk about their feelings regarding the treatment. Although she made no attempt to interpret what went on in this little group, she was able to offer reassurance and to determine which patients were most upset and might need a mild sedative in order to sleep. Personnel on the morning shift began to notice a change in the attitude of shock patients and had little or no difficulty in getting them to cooperate with the routine of treatment.

On another ward, a night shift aide early in the morning visited each patient whose name appeared on the E.S.T. list. He would awaken him by sitting on the side of the bed a few moments and chatting with him, all the while carefully appraising his physical condition. He urged the patient to wash his face, hands and teeth and to go to the bathroom. He made sure that the patient was dressed in a loose-fitting robe, and that when he arrived in the day hall to await treatment, there was an interesting program on the television. If one of his patients seemed to be particularly upset, he stayed close by, answering questions patiently and honestly. He was careful to report to the day nurse a patient who appeared to be physically ill, or a patient who was particularly overactive or underactive. This group of patients, like those in the previous example, were much less fearful, and other personnel who took over had less uphill work in getting them to go for treatment.

Still another project can be described concerning the actual period of the giving of treatment. This project was carried on during the summer months by a group of young college students. These men, in the process of educating themselves to religious endeavor, took particular interest in patients receiving E.S.T. Each morning they accompanied patients to the shock unit, stayed with them in the waiting room and were present as they awakened. The students brought in a phonograph and played a continuous assortment of semi-classical records. Their quiet listening and diversified conversation did much to relieve tension in the waiting room. Patients recognized them in the recovery room and did not feel quite so alone. During the day, these same students circulated among the different wards joining in patient activities and offering religious solace wherever it was needed. The shock unit experienced a smoothly functioning summer.

The aforementioned are samples of what can be accomplished by only a little extra effort. The success or the failure of electric shock therapy depends on many people who are actively involved in it. The aide plays an extremely important role in terms of *support, reassurance* and *comfort.*

Occupational Therapy

Those who are acquainted with mental hospitals usually associate the term "occupational therapy" with "craft shops" or specially equipped rooms set aside for daily programs of metal work, wood carving, bead stringing, and so on. Although this is a true picture, it is not nearly complete, for occupational therapy encompasses many other activities conducted in other areas than the occupational therapy shops. The role of the aide in the implementation of occupational therapy is a too-long neglected one, and at the present time nursing personnel and O.T. workers are attempting to outline adjunctive functions for aides which will be of maximum benefit to patients. In many hospitals, for example, the primary duty of the aide in relation to occupational therapy is escorting patients to and from various activities or, perhaps, staying with a disturbed patient while he is in the O.T. shop.

As mentioned in Chapter 1 of this book, occupational therapy is prescribed for patients by the doctor. It is conducted in O.T. shops, on the wards and in various industrial units by trained occupational therapists. In the industrial occupational therapy units (laundry, greenhouse, cafeterias, etc.), the actual work of patients is done under the supervision of those persons in charge of the industry, or by workers trained in industrial therapy.

Work selected for and produced by patients should be primarily for their benefit, and patients are not assigned to tasks in order to fill hospital needs. Aides, by actively joining O.T. conferences at which doctors, nurses and occupational therapists are present, can frequently offer valuable suggestions regarding patients' special aptitudes or preferences. It is important, also, that the aide encourage his patient, whatever his project may be The patient needs support and reassurance, and he needs appreciation for his efforts, no matter how minimal they are at first. He wants people to be interested in his creative efforts, particularly his friend the aide. The aide can do much to help the patient who is assigned to industrial therapy. He can make sure that the patient gets up, is properly dressed and fed, and arrives at "work" on time. He can talk to the patient about his "job." Often, through such conversations, information will come to light which may indicate that a different assignment is desirable. Patients sometimes build feelings of resentment because they are not "paid" for their work around the hospital. This particular problem often falls to the aide for solution, for such resistance usually appears as the patient is about to go to work in the morning, or when he returns from work, tired, in the late afternoon. Somehow it is hard for the patient to accept the aide's explanation that he is receiving much more benefit from his work than mere pay would provide. That this is part of his progress toward better mental health, and ultimate return to his family and the community, is not always enough for the patient. As mentioned in Chapter 1, today many patients *are* paid for the work they do, both in the hospital and on the outside.

In many large, public mental hospitals, there are still not enough occupational therapists to reach all the patients. Consequently, administrators and doctors are troubled as they go about the wards and see row after row of patients, unoccupied, sitting staring into space or quarreling among themselves for lack of something better to do. A group of patients receiving occupational therapy of some sort are less troubled to ward personnel in terms of management problems. There is at least a partial answer to this institutional bugaboo, but it has not yet been developed to anywhere near its full potentiality. The answer is that aides and nurses, working day by day on the wards with patients can start and continue occupational therapy projects. Materials, instruction and direction can be provided by the occupational therapist, but the actual initiation of the project and its continuation can be carried through by the ward personnel.

One state hospital aide, older and rather heavily built, had been told by her doctor that she must limit her work considerably or else she would seriously endanger her health. She became quite depressed about this since she knew no other work, and yet felt that she would be letting her fellow employees down if she did not continue to carry her share of the work load. She worked in a ward of senile old ladies who seemed to be unusually destructive. Every day several sheets, blankets and dresses would be torn to shreds, completely unsalvageable. One morning she noticed an old lady braiding pieces of rag together and making circular mats out of them. The thought occurred to her that the destructiveness on her ward could be turned into useful occupation for her patients. She conferred with the head occupational therapist who agreed to see that bags of unsalvageable material were sent to the ward each day, and also agreed to teach the aide the art of making rag rugs. After receiving final approval from the ward doctor, the aide painstakingly began her work. After breakfast in the morning, she would gather the patients in a circle in the day hall and have them tear strips for the rug-making. She showed them how to start their rugs, and she and the occupational therapist spent extra time with patients who were slow to catch on or had poor eyesight or some other physical incapacity. Her co-workers, happy that the patients were occupied and that they could get their housecleaning done and untidy patients taken care of, appreciated her efforts, thus relieving her of the idea that she was "not doing her share."

This is only one example of how aides can make their own work easier by adding to the diversional and productive activities on their wards under the direction of the occupational therapists. Often, overactivity can be channeled into productive activity with the introduction of simple, energy-releasing tasks such as carting linen, moving beds, or washing down walls. Such tasks certainly are diversional, and they are also therapeutic, for a patient who can start a job and do it well becomes an asset to his group rather than a liability.

Recreational Therapy

There are large hospitals that still have no official recreational director to provide indoor and outdoor recreational activities for patients. Most patient dances, picnics, ball games and the like are sponsored by either the occupational therapy department or groups of volunteers from the surrounding community. In either case, aides assume an important role, since they must accompany and supervise their patients and usually must become participants also. Recreational therapy for patients is really a part of everyone's job and provides a number of opportunities to promote the mental health of the patient. For one thing, the sense of competition is strong in all of us and is a normal part of everyday life. Recreational activities provide a medium for social contacts and are, in a sense, a convenient outlet for aggressive or hostile feelings. A particularly noisy and self-centered patient insisted on pitching at a ward game one afternoon. Because of his boisterousness and apparent conceit, he was not well liked by the other patients. The "gallery" took full advantage of his every mistake, yelling "throw the pitcher out" and similar derogatory remarks. The patient later discussed with his doctor his feelings about the episode, stating that he had never fully realized before how his braggart actions must affect other people. At the same time, his fellow patients felt that they had been a bit too hard on him and went out of their way to be nice to him afterward. Personnel noted a definite improvement in his attitude, and from that day forward he began to make progress toward recovery.

Overactive patients will usually participate in recreational activities without much urging. The underactive patient, in contrast, presents a much more difficult problem to the aide. He is usually so absorbed in himself, so drained of energy, that there is little that interests him. Starting with a simple ward recreation such as checkers, usually he can be persuaded to try a hand at ping-pong or "catch." It is important to keep in mind that often his depression is the result of feelings of unworthiness, and for this reason it is sometimes necessary to make sure that he comes out the victor. Once he feels his own capability in competition, he may become a tough match. The physical exercise involved in most games will make him feel better, too, plus the necessary "mixing" with other people.

On picnics, patients like to help with the work—gathering wood, carrying food, ice, etc., and actually cooking the hot dogs. How dull the picnic is for patients when they must sit in a limited, well-supervised area and be served their food by the personnel! The same holds true for ward parties. Patients like to help with the decorations, making the ward look as presentable as possible, serving refreshments, calling square dances, initiating parlor games, or demonstrating any other special talents that they might possess.

Recreational activities somehow seem closer to community and home life than almost any other opportunity that the hospital presents to the patient. Aides soon learn the value of simple ward games, walks outside, ward softball teams, bowling, and coed dances.

Industrial Therapy

In the section on occupational therapy, industrial therapy has already been mentioned. However, in the past few years this particular area of psychiatric treatment has assumed much more importance as a *therapeutic tool,* and the psychiatric aide will need to be up to date on the various aspects of industrial therapy.

For many years, "patient labor" was used in mental hospitals. Most of these hospitals could not have functioned without patient workers. During World War II, some hospitals were so pathetically short of help that certain patients were given keys and acted as ward attendants. This type of patient work could not be honored with the title, "Industrial Therapy," because its purpose was to help the hospital and not the patient.

Today when the patient begins to improve, the physician may ask the person in charge of industrial therapy to investigate the patient's work background and to begin to think of a suitable and *healthful* work assignment for him. It is important to note that, in some instances, a patient's former work might *not* be healthful for him. This factor is considered along with (1) the patient's capacity to work in relation to the progress of his recovery and (2) his future work prospects upon his return to the community. A large mental hospital offers an amazing variety of job opportunities for industrial therapy—kitchen, laundry, carpenter shop, farm and dairy work, electrician work, canning, sewing, housework, to mention only a few.

In the beginning, the patient is "paid" for his work in terms of therapeutic benefit. However, as the patient gets better, he is paid a regular salary which is placed in his account and often gives him a good financial start when he is discharged or sent to a foster home or "half-way house."

As previously mentioned, industrial therapy is usually in

the charge of one person whose job includes keeping up-to-date lists of job openings and lists of patients ready to work. He also makes frequent visits to patients on the job and keeps notes on the progress he observes during these visits. He attends all meetings held by the physician for industrial therapists and allied groups. Unofficial industrial "therapists" are the persons in charge of the various departments of the hospital where the business of hospital *maintenance* goes on.

The psychiatric aide has a responsibility in all this, too. Because of his consistent friendly contact with the patients in his ward, he is often the first to recognize when a patient is willing and able to work. He often knows what a patient wants to do and the type of work for which he is best suited. It is usually the aide in whom the patient confides when he is dissatisfied with his job placement or is assigned to a job which is still too much for him in relation to his illness. In his vital role as part of the psychiatric team, the aide can convey such information to the physician and others involved in this ever-growing, constructive and positive therapeutic method.

Some Therapies No Longer in Common Use

With the increased use of psychotherapy and tranquilizers, the formerly popular therapies such as electric shock treatment, insulin therapy, hydrotherapy, and hypnosis are now used very rarely. Narcotherapy and lobotomy are two methods of treatment that have virtually gone out of use entirely. Also, there is the increased emphasis on community mental health programs where most of these treatments are not used. The aide is referred to older texts or to his hospital's procedure book, if such treatments are still in use at his hospital.

Introduction

Part of his job responsibility was concerned with housekeeping and maintenance. It brought to mind his own struggle to obtain a home, and what his home meant to him and to his family. Because mental patients stay hospitalized so much longer than other kinds of patients, the hospital necessarily becomes their home—sometimes for many, many years. What goes into a house besides timbers, metal, wires and shingles to make it a HOME? Comfortable furniture, curtains, pictures—but what else? Some of the prettiest houses are not homes *but remain only houses. The* people *in the house can make it a home. And he was one of the people who lived in the hospital-house, at least part of the time. What could he do to make it a real home for his patients?*

PART 1

Your Ward Is Home for the Patients

Cleanliness

In some large mental hospitals, keeping the wards clean is the responsibility of a special housekeeping department. In most, however, the bulk of this job falls to the aides. It can get to be the most time-consuming task if allowed to be so, and although this may result in a scrupulously clean ward, it is doubtful whether or not patients will be contented or will get well as rapidly as they might. Cleanliness is extremely important to the well-being of most people, and there is no doubt that patients' living quarters should be kept as clean as possible, but not at the expense of all other activities. It is true that many patient buildings are old and cumbersome; it is true that many wards are large and contain from 75 to 100 human beings; it is true that more frequently than not cleaning supplies are hard to get and hard to keep. These factors may make the job of cleaning seem insurmountable. As with most therapy (and cleanliness is as much a therapy as any previously mentioned specialized treatments) much depends upon the individuals involved. An aide who maintains a clean personal appearance and takes pride in the cleanliness of his own home is going to do a good job of housekeeping on his ward. And the same goes for patients! Some patients may be too sick temporarily to care about their appearance or the appearance of their surroundings, but others *do* care and will offer to help and will follow through with considerable assistance. Still other patients are too concerned with cleanliness, and their activities have to be curbed somewhat; others may need considerable encouragement to help with ward work. Either way, such activities can be very beneficial for patients, and patients should have a part in daily cleaning activities. It is true that occasionally a patient's zeal is capitalized on, and he is "used" far beyond what he should be. In some instances, a patient's stay in the hospital may be lengthened, because he contributes such valuable service that personnel feel that they cannot do without him. This, of course, is poor reasoning and is certainly very unfair to the patient.

The aide constantly has to combat dust, grime, trash, and odors. Floors need to be done each day, and the same with lavatories and tub rooms. Walls need to be washed down, furniture (including beds) cleaned, and windows washed—not every day except in a specific incident of soiling—but frequently enough to make the job a routine rather than an overwhelming one. Whether or not special preparations are available for cleaning, soap and water still remain the most useful and ready cleansers. Some walls will need washing every day, if there is a particularly untidy patient or a patient who is going through a phase of smearing feces. Incidentally, one of the best methods that aides suggest to one another for handling this particular problem is to get the untidy patient to help clean the room. If he is simply not able in the beginning, at least have him present while the job is being done.

The aide can talk to the patient about it, as he would to a partner, in terms of the increased work involved, the unpleasant odors and the easier solution of asking to go to the bathroom.

Cleanliness implies much more, of course, than only floors and furniture and windows. Clean clothing, clean bed linen, and clean mattresses and pillows are vitally important. Even if these are properly taken care of, it is still a waste of energy unless the patient himself is clean. Cleanliness of the human body involves more than a bath or a shower. It means cut and cleaned fingernails and toenails; clean heads, free of lice; teeth brushed frequently and kept in good repair; underarms and faces shaved whenever necessary. Recently, a group of aides working in a large, untidy building adopted the idea of bringing in their bathing suits on shower days and going right into the showers with regressed patients. They made it a full-scale operation, scrubbing ears, shaving underarms, doing nails and, if any kind of lice were present, immediately starting proper treatment for getting rid of the lice. They enlisted the aid of some of their "better" patients who also got into the showers with patients who did not help themselves, dried patients, helped them to dress and combed their hair.

An unhealthy odor in a ward is excusable in only one instance—when the place has old, wooden floors. Such floors are sometimes time-soaked with urine, spilled food, and so on, and all the scrubbing possible does not seem to improve the situation. However, even this can be helped by bringing in the maintenance men to sand the floors for revarnishing. It is amazing what a difference a little fresh paint can make in a room or a ward. And painting can be done by patients working along with the aide. Patients get very enthusiastic about such projects, and the improved appearance of things creates an increased desire on the part of patients to *keep* them nice. Chipped, stained beds are an eyesore and never seem really clean. The same is true of walls. If the hospital painters are busy with another project the aide can try to obtain paint (and advice!) from them and set to work in his own ward. All the personnel—and patients—should have a say as to the color wanted, and the choice of color can become a very important point. It is well to keep in mind that whatever color is chosen may have to be lived with for a *long* time.

If toilets, urinals, wash basins and shower walls are scrubbed frequently, patients tend to develop much healthier habits of personal hygiene. This is particularly true in the very untidy wards; it brings to mind the fact that there does not need to be an "untidy ward" if the whole ward team works together to eliminate that nickname.

One more point about ward cleanliness. Many hospital administrators are plagued with the headache of the constant "battle between the shifts." Each shift of personnel thinks that it has the hardest job in one sense or another; each shift blames the other for an "untidy" ward or a "problem" patient or for disappearing supplies! Of course, one solution is overlapping time schedules so that the members of the two changing shifts are on the ward together for a little while. A more mature, healthy solution would be a recognition of and respect for the implied duties which *each* shift has to perform. For example, in relation to cleaning, there is no reason why the first or day shift has to do all the patient bathing, head cleaning, etc. Nor should they be expected to do all the window washing, floor polishing or changing of linen. In Part 2 it will be pointed out that each ward *can* organize its work so that tasks will be distributed fairly evenly. The basic knowledge that the patient comes first, that the job is to take care of the patient, and that because of personnel, supply, and time shortages, aides and others have to work *together* rather than against each other should eliminate rivalry and jealousy between shifts.

Maintenance

Maintenance, in general, means "upkeep," and it is logical that it should follow the section on cleanliness. Although the aide is not expected to be a "jack-of-all-trades"—that is, plumber, electrician and carpenter—it is his responsibility to see that repairs are made in these job areas as soon as possible. In the home, when a fuse blows or the sink gets stopped up, or there is a loose piece of tile in the kitchen floor, we set to work and do something about it. If we know how to replace a fuse and have one handy, we set to work and do it right away. It is inconvenient to be without lights. In the ward, it is the same way. Window panes get broken, fuses blow, toilets get plugged up and overflow, tiles get loose or ripped up, locks and keys get broken, and so on.

Most mental hospitals have personnel who specialize in repairing and replacing where necessary—plumber, carpenter and electrician. Unless these people know about maintenance needs, they cannot care for them. Thus, the aide, upon discovering a maintenance need, sets about caring for it as soon as possible. In most hospitals a written requisition is needed, but if the situation is urgent, a phone call to the proper place, *followed* by a written requisition, usually will accomplish the task. It is important that the aide notify the head nurse or the supervising nurse in such emergencies, too, since she is required to know the needs in areas for which she is responsible.

Broken windows create various hazards, such as jagged edges, unhealthy drafts, or encouragement for escape. In special units for adolescents, this has become a serious problem. A dislodged tile or two may tempt a destructive patient to "finish the job." A stopped-up, overflowing toilet is untidy and a definite health hazard. Lack of lights in certain areas of the ward may frighten patients and even endanger personnel and patients. In the dark, a frightened, confused patient may assault someone, attempt suicide or try to escape. A vivid incident comes to mind of a patient who succeeded in hanging himself over the foot of his bed during a "blackout" resulting from a faulty fuse which was not replaced immediately.

The subject of maintenance should include care and upkeep of available supplies. A broken polisher does no good sitting in a closet somewhere; a television set that is not working gives patients no benefit; old, smelly mops make extra work, as do broken broom handles, leaks in the pipes, or badly torn laundry bags. Whatever the system for issuing supplies, the aide has to make his needs *known*. If supplies are hard to obtain, then he has to use every effort to conserve what he does have. A wet, dirty mop deteriorates much faster than one that is cleaned, rinsed and preferably left outdoors to dry. Patients who are very cold because of a rash of broken window panes or broken window sashes will create more problems than those who live in a ward where proper ventilation is maintained—but not by accident.

Thus, ward maintenance is a responsibility of the aide and thence of those specialized persons upon whom he calls for assistance. Again, all three shifts of personnel are responsible for maintenance, as they are for cleanliness.

The Intangibles

By far the most important factor involved in making the ward more homelike for the patient and the personnel is that of the intangible things that can be present. In one of the former chapters it was mentioned that there is a *felt* difference in atmosphere as one moves from ward to ward; that some wards seem to be in a continual uproar, while others systematically maintain a healthful, or therapeutic, atmosphere. Specifically, wherein do the differences lie? First and most important, in the *attitudes* of personnel toward patients, and vice versa. A review of Chapter 2 might bring more clearly to mind the elements involved in the establishment of therapeutic attitudes. Many times this healthful attitude is expressed by small evidences that personnel really care for patients and, in turn, that patients really care what goes into their immediate environment. For example, pictures placed, homemade rugs in the day hall, magazines and newspapers available, flowers or well-cared-for plants on the window-sills or tables. An aide proudly tells of his work on a ward that had been regarded as the most disturbed in the men's acute service. "We asked for drapes a year ago and were told that we couldn't have them, for they wouldn't last a week! After much persistence and persuasion, we finally got the drapes. We are the only ward in the building that can say that our drapes have not been torn down this past year. And, I might add, neither personnel nor supervision has been increased." Thus, the horrified objection, "Plants! On a disturbed ward? That's dangerous! They'd be thrown in a moment!" Experience has demonstrated that this is not true. The nicer the environment and the things placed in it for the benefit of patients, the fewer the problems. Patients in a disturbed unit in a distant hospital recently heard from were given large window boxes and were asked to care for them. One patient produced two rows of very good radishes that spring. Other patients have asked if they could plant a garden in the yard in back of their building. Obviously, these patients are not left idle; the nurses and the aides keep them busy enough to eliminate the desire to destroy pictures, magazines or their window boxes.

Once in a while ward personnel get a bit overly enthusiastic about added attractions around their wards. This may give patients a feeling of overcrowdedness (as in a small home into which too many "gimmicks" have been introduced). Too many pictures, plants, rugs, etc., make cleaning problems more complicated also.

Too much emphasis cannot be laid on the importance of

the *attitudes* prevalent on the ward. The importance of the role that the aide plays—whether it be substitute mother, father, sister, brother, friend, teacher, or what—and his mature fulfillment of his patients' needs is vital to his function as a "homemaker" for his patients.

PART 2

Organizing Your Work

Schedules for Activities and Daily Care

One of the major signs of the onset of mental illness is confusion. Disorganization of thought, apparent carelessness and disregard for everyday routine are very common with the newly ill person, and the person who is chronically ill, and very sick. Some patients stay up all night and sleep most of the day. Others pay little or no attention to the details of daily living, such as brushing teeth, combing hair, dressing tidily and eating regularly. Still others will "reverse" the usual and decide to do laundry at 2 or 3 o'clock in the morning, or may want to go for a walk at midnight. Thus, one can look upon routine and organization as healthful patterns of living for most people, and it should be a goal toward which the aide works in his daily care of his patients.

Needless to say, some people "overorganize." They live by time limits and written notes, keep budgets accounting for every penny and observe the details of their personal hygiene minutely. There is a happy medium, and it can be initiated and followed through by aides so that the ward runs smoothly and efficiently, and patients are learning, over again, how to manage themselves.

Keeping a schedule makes the job easier. Without some routine, things pile up and ward personnel get so swamped that tasks seem to be always ahead of them and never behind. This can be very discouraging and easily promotes an "I don't care, what can you do?" attitude among personnel and patients. There are certain things that must be done daily; others that must be done weekly; and others, monthly. A convenient, comfortable schedule in which everyone participates and does his share is a much simpler proposition than a hodge-podge of miscellaneous tasks assigned hurriedly and sometimes with irritation. Certain basic patient needs—bathing, shaving, dressing and feeding—are daily responsibilities for all ward personnel. Additionally, patients need exercise, diversion, and friendly, personal attention.

Special therapies may be prescribed daily for some patients, or perhaps three times a week for others. Various clinics are held on special days. Ward personnel should know about these care activities and can easily familiarize themselves with them, so that it is not necessary to run to the ward bulletin board or the head nurse for reminders. However, this does not mean that schedules are not posted or that specific assignments are not given. On the contrary, schedules can be posted in a spot convenient to all personnel, and such schedules should be *kept up to date*. The head nurse or charge aide can conserve everybody's time and energy by making definite and fair assignments. If enough personnel are on duty, it is wise to leave one person relatively free, since dozens of different errands come up during each and every day. If no one is specifically responsible for them, one aide or another must be taken from his assigned job and sent off here and there, thus delaying and sometimes even eliminating his assigned tasks. For example, a patient may have to go to the x-ray laboratory, and that department is housed several buildings away. It takes considerable time to transport the patient back and forth, and he may have to wait his turn for the x-ray picture. Thus, an aide might be gone from the ward (and his regular assignment) for one or two hours, and there is seldom anyone to take over for him.

Making *fair* assignments is extremely important for ward morale. Too many times the bickering between shifts is directly related to the fact that one shift thinks that the other has less work to do. A supervisor recently related this story which illustrates the problem. The building involved had one barber for 175 patients (some buildings have no barber) so that the responsibility of shaving patients had been largely taken over by the aides and the nurses on the day shift. With increasing activities during the day, the shaving process slipped noticeably, and patients were untidy and uncomfortable much of the time. When the afternoon personnel were approached with the assignment of shaving patients, the attitude expressed was: "If we start that the day shift will get the idea it's *our* job and won't do any shaving." Obviously, something is wrong when *sharing* a task is resented. Sadly enough, the patient is the one who suffers—he still goes unshaved.

All shifts can take equal responsibility for seeing that the basic needs of patients are met. It is true that there are different kinds of duties at different times of day, and some are more time-consuming than others. The evening shift personnel can bathe some patients (particularly the more untidy ones) before they go to bed, and likewise, the night shift can bathe some patients when they arise in the morning. Accepting the assignment of patients, by name, to be bathed by each shift might equalize the responsibility better. The same routine can be followed for shaves.

In discussing the fairness of assignments, it can also be

mentioned that certain aides do not always have the same jobs to do. Some jobs give more pleasure and satisfaction than others. For example, in one large hospital, patients frequently go to big league baseball games as part of their recreational program. It is essential that they be accompanied by aides. Certainly, this duty can be fairly distributed among the aides during the summer. In some wards, the major responsibilities of the aides are cleaning the ward and supervising patients. Nowadays "supervision" of patients does not necessarily mean standing guard at the doorway, but, rather playing cards or talking with patients, at the same time keeping an alert eye on all that goes on in the area. The physical labor involved in housecleaning earmarks it as a task that can be shifted around among the personnel at stated intervals.

Here is another point regarding the fairness of assignment and organization which any leader such as the charge aide, the head nurse or the supervisor will do well to remember: one cannot assign a task that he or she would not do if the need arose. Much of successful leadership is based on the ability to set a good example by *doing*.

Keeping Track of Your Patients

Patients come to a mental hospital when they can no longer keep track of themselves and their belongings, and when others find it impossible to fulfill this function for them. Often patients will grow to accept this responsibility for themselves as they slip into hospital routines. However, the fact remains that many depend on the hospital personnel to provide personal guidance for them for many years. In a sense, the mental hospital is not only a protection for the community but also a protection for the patient, and he needs this kind of security.

Most hospitals attempt to create an atmosphere of normal living for patients. Such an atmosphere includes work and play and relaxing social contact. Hospitals are still hospitals and are obligated to have knowledge of patients' whereabouts at all times. Thus, the necessity for a few locked wards and enclosed yards, and supervision of activities. One of the things that a person values highly is his personal privacy. Unhappily, there is little or no privacy in the large mental hospital. Recognition of the patients' *need* for privacy helps the aide in his attempt to maintain, as much as possible, a subtle approach to his job of keeping track of patients. There is no doubt that patients resent the person who uses his keys as a psychological weapon or has to shout and be "bossy" in order to maintain routine. Kindness can do more than all the shouting and threats in the world. The aide who has gained the confidence and the friendship of his patients does not usually have a group of restless patients constantly looking for ways to escape or hide or do away with themselves.

The previous section has mentioned the use of posted schedules as a means of making everyone's work easier. The same holds true in relation to the maintenance of up-to-date lists of patients who go to various regular, planned activities, who are actively suicidal, or are allowed numerous privileges. Such lists are not maintained to create a jail-like atmosphere but to *help* those whose job it is to know the whereabouts of patients. New aides and students often are the "victims" of the clever patient who will stand at the door and say, "Oh, I have ground privileges. You can let me out!" This is the time to ask someone who knows, or, if no one is around, to review the list of privileged patients and be sure rather than sorry. When taking patients walking, to meals, to the movies or to some other function, the aide can count them without being obvious about it. There is a need for counting. An aide gives a good illustration, as follows: he was accompanying a group of old men to the cafeteria one evening. He did not bother to count. Later, when putting his patients to bed, he discovered one missing. The missing patient was blind but had been around the hospital many years and knew his way on the grounds. "I didn't know what to do," the aide said. "He was a favorite of ours, and I was worried sick. I called the supervisor and we searched everywhere to no avail. Tom was missing for two days, and I never spent a more miserable period of time. We organized a search party and finally found him down in the abandoned orchard. He had made himself a little camp; he was hungry but otherwise all right. How fortunate that it was summer!"

Another incident that occurred recently in a nearby hospital involved a suicidal patient who had actively resisted therapy for some time. One morning she could not be found anywhere. The aide who had been assigned to stay with her had gone to the rest room and had not asked that someone keep an eye on the patient during her absence. Personnel were sure she had not left the ward, but a thorough investigation of possible hiding places did not reveal her. Finally, after several hours, she emerged on her own from an old ventilator. She had discovered that the grating covering the opening was loose and had squeezed herself up into the ventilator and pulled the grating back into place. She had even taken some bread with her! This incident was amusing in a sense, for the patient had outwitted everyone, but it could have been tragic.

The aide who familiarizes himself with his patients and knows their general habits finds it easy to keep track of them, and, in turn, his patients feel secure.

Ward Rounds

"Ward rounds" is a term used to indicate different things in different places. In some hospitals it means the doctor's visit to the ward each day or once a week. As used in this text, it means trips back and forth throughout the ward made by nursing personnel during each day and night. At certain times, these trips should be systematic. For instance, at the beginning of each shift when responsibility for patients' welfare changes hands, personnel taking over must make sure that all is in order before personnel leaving the ward are dismissed.

A short conference can be held, and any special problems can be made known to the relieving charge personnel at this time. Then, the person or persons coming on duty can walk through the ward with the person or persons going off duty, making sure to check the following: (1) the presence and the well-being of *all* patients, (2) the *cleanliness* of the ward in general, (3) any special *maintenance* difficulty such as a stopped-up toilet, a broken lock, or an escape hazard and (4) facts concerning any new admission, particular behavior problem or physical illness, accompanied by specific doctor's orders. If all these things are attended to, responsibility will also be in order.

To illustrate the importance of this principle that the change of shifts make complete rounds *together*, a doctor tells this incident: "One night I was on first call and had just gone to sleep when the phone rang. The aide on Ward 8 told me, in a frantic voice, that a patient had hung himself—to come right over. When I arrived, I found the patient hanging over the foot of his bed, a piece of neatly torn sheet around his neck, and tied over the foot of the bed to the bed spring. He appeared to be dead, but we worked over him for a long time. We were not able to save him, and an investigation was held. We were not proud of what was revealed. Several reliable patients told us that the patient had worked, uninterrupted, very quietly tearing the sheet for more than two hours. During all this time he was not disturbed by personnel, who remained in the ward office from the time they finished putting patients to bed until the night shift reported for duty. Apparently, he had hung himself after other patients in his dormitory had fallen asleep. He had been dead only about a half hour. He was first discovered by a fellow patient who had gotten up to go to the bathroom. Because no rounds had been made at 11 o'clock by both shifts, we could not pin the blame anywhere. But all of those aides should have had him on their conscience!"

Particularly careful supervision involving frequent rounds is essential after patients have retired for the night. It is during the hours of dark that patients are most likely to harm themselves or one another, or to attempt escape. Fires can gain more headway at night, patients on tranquilizing drugs may have a serious toxic reaction, and patients are lonely and fearful in the dark.

In the daytime, while going about routine duties, aides can watch over their patients. Patients receiving special treatments should be observed as often as possible. Patients in seclusion or those who have been sedated need constant attention. Often, because there is not enough help, this is not practical. But these patients are a serious responsibility and should be observed at every opportunity.

Extra Errands

What are the extra errands that come up every day? Routine is constantly being interrupted in the large, active mental hospital. Patients must be transported here and there; patients have accidents; they must be helped to bathe and dress for visitors, or for church services. Sometimes aides have to relieve workers on other wards, help out in the operating room, or leave the grounds to help pick up a strayed patient. Occasionally, aides are asked to help demonstrate or teach new medical students, nursing students or new aides. Sometimes the hospital sponsors special events requiring extra supervision and companionship for patients.

All of these things come under the heading of extra errands

or special tasks that are not included in the everyday run of things.

Whether these extra errands are pleasant or unpleasant, aides can take turns carrying them through. This idea blends with the principle of *sharing*, which is so important when the load is top-heavy as in our understaffed and overcrowded mental hospitals. Unwillingness or lack of cooperation not only makes the job tougher but adds to the feeling that many patients have that they are a burden to those caring for them. Patients frequently have this feeling at home while getting sick, and no doubt it adds to their illness. We who care for them can at least try to let them know that it is important and worthwhile to us that they get well. If doing extra tasks helps in their ultimate progress it is all right with us!

Introduction

He was beginning to feel more and more secure in his job. At the same time he recognized in himself a growing interest in patients as people. He began to see his part in the scheme of things, and often responsibility lay heavy on his shoulders. More and more he was using initiative and originality in his work, and this gave him a sense of accomplishment. Many emergency situations arose on his ward as the weeks rolled into months. He was grateful for the first-aid hints that he had picked up while working in the special therapy units, and for the awareness, also acquired there, of physical ills. He had occasion to take patients to church, and he marveled at their good behavior. He experienced losing a patient and spent a number of bad hours until his patient was returned. He began to feel seasoned, and he liked the feeling.

Emergencies and Special Problems

A mental hospital is a community within itself. The kinds of things that occur in the mental hospital are akin to the kinds of things that occur wherever a large number of people live and work together. Everyday emergencies arise, sometimes minor and sometimes major, and it is usually the aide who must meet and handle the emergencies immediately. Thus, every effort should be made to develop alertness and stability, for both are urgently needed in the face of crisis. Frequently, mental patients are so ill that they cannot report accidents or injury to themselves or others, and the aide shoulders a large responsibility to his patients in maintaining constant observation of their welfare.

This chapter will discuss the various kinds of happenings, on and off the ward, that constitute emergency situations and will offer general suggestions as to the management of such occasions. Each heading, listed in order of its importance, represents a situation which can be either a small or a great emergency. In a mental hospital, where doors may be locked, and certainly where many of the people involved cannot assume responsibility for themselves, *every* emergency becomes an event of major importance.

Fire

Every so often one reads a newspaper account of a fire in a mental hospital or nursing home. Usually, such incidents are vividly described, and an old building, many patients—some feeble, others childlike—locked doors and the absence of sufficient help result in tragic endings. Heroic efforts are made, but there is still the photograph of windows, lighted through the night by flame, and with a solitary figure hunched here and there against the light.

From the time we first burn ourselves with matches or on a hot stove, we have a dread of fire. Such instinctive dread of fire becomes complicated by *fear* when a fire is not *controlled*. Fear is oftentime the real killer in a serious fire, for it causes people to run pell-mell in every direction, to forget their fellow men and to jump and fall and fight their way to freedom from smoke and flame.

Any fire in the mental hospital constitutes a major emergency and should be treated as such. Of course, smoking is the greatest hazard, even in hospitals where smoking rules are rigidly planned and enforced. There are many other sources of fire: faulty electric wiring, overheated ventilators, accumulations of old rags and newspapers, refrigerator motors, sterilizers, even lightning. Most hospitals have their own specific rules for reporting and dealing with fires, but some general considerations hold for aides to remember. Even a very small fire should be reported *immediately* to a designated central communication point. *Above all else*, the safety of the patient comes first. The aide is not only up against the problem of handling some patients who are confused and uncooperative, but he is faced with the problem of fear. Knowing, *ahead of time*, the location of exits in his ward, he can lead his patients away from the fire out of doors or into another building. The aide who knows his patient well can enlist the help of a group of cooperative patients for this detail. If there is sufficient help available, the charge aide or the nurse can designate an aide to use first extinguishers, if necessary, and to close windows and doors which may be creating a draft around the fire area. *Let those whose job it specifically*

Patients can't always tell you.

is handle the fire itself. In most hospitals, all hands respond to a fire alarm, and in a matter of minutes reserve personnel arrive to deal with putting out the fire, closing windows, etc. *The aide's job is directly with his patients and their safety.* Hospital property is and should be secondary to human life.

The situation differs and assumes greater gravity when a fire breaks out in an area where patients are not ambulatory. Since, in many large mental hospitals, from a third to a half of the patients fall into the category of feeble (old people), bed-fast or chair-bound, it is extremely important to be able to deal with a fire emergency among these patients. Again, patients are of prime importance, and in this crisis it is particularly urgent that the aide maintain a clear head. Moving bed patients takes much longer than filing a group of ambulatory patients out of danger. All usable exits should be opened. The number of standard stretchers kept on a ward would not begin to answer the need in a major fire. Thus, a competent person can organize teams of two or four persons (depending on the weight of the patient), to grasp the *under sheet* at each corner and carry the patient, bedclothes and all, to safety. In severely cold weather, those in charge should designate a safety point, either within the immediate building or a building close by, since it would be hazardous to take such patients out of doors for more than a few minutes.

This discussion of the aide's responsibility during a fire has been very general. As with any emergency, the situation will always differ in some respects. Much depends on the number of personnel available, the amount (and condition) of equipment available, the construction of buildings, including the number of usable exits (an exit into a narrow winding stairway would be useless in a real fire) and the aide's familiarity with the fire rules of his own hospital. Frequent fire drills help keep both personnel and equipment "up to date." If the aide remains calm enough to remember two vital points—

report *any* fire *immediately,* and take care of *patients* first— tragedy can be prevented.

Suicide

Any mental patient is a potential suicide. That is, whether or not he is marked "Suicidal," whether or not he has ever attempted suicide before, whether or not he is depressed, whether or not he expresses suicidal thoughts, he may still attempt to kill himself. He is mentally ill; therefore his behavior cannot be accurately predicted. Suicide, like fire, is a constant hazard in a mental hospital. It is surprising, considering the *kind* of community a mental hospital constitutes, that the number of suicides among hospitalized patients is quite low. There are several reasons for this, but certainly a creditable one is the alert observation of patients as carried out by the aides.

Sometimes, patients are admitted to the ward as "actively suicidal," and the nurses and the aides have specific instructions to follow regarding observation of that particular patient. More often, the aide does not find out that a patient is suicidal until much later, and he must rely on his own knowledge and observation of the patient's behavior as his warning that the patient is suicidal. The aide learns to recognize the patient's need to be alone, his meaningful remarks—usually against himself, his interest in the location of "sharps," cleaning and disinfectant fluids, and the hours when the "shifts" change; he notices a patient's degree of depression (a profoundly depressed patient usually does not have the energy or the initiative to perform a suicidal act), and patients who conceal tableware, bits of glass, leather belts, etc. He watches such patients with more than the usual interest and keeps them within his knowledge at all times.

Patients attempt suicide in various ways. Some methods are more common than others, as, for example, hanging (bathrobe cord, belt, necktie, sheet) and the cutting of the wrists or the throat or both (glass, razor, broken spoon, nail). If left alone long enough, a patient may try to drown himself in the bathtub or by putting his head in the toilet bowl. Other methods include burning by setting fire to bedclothes, suffocating in bedclothes, drinking or eating poison, saving drugs until a lethal dose is acquired, refusing to eat; patients have even been known to succeed in killing themselves by throwing themselves head-first from a ledge, or the head of the bed!

Prevention of suicide is, of course, the best remedy to the problem. Knowing the whereabouts and the activities of all his patients is the first responsibility of the aide. If the aide knows, either by his observation of the patient's behavior or from the report of the nurse or the doctor, that a patient is suicidal, he pays special attention, tries to divert his patient, tries to keep him with a group of patients, locates his bed either in a dormitory with other patients, or in the hall where observation is always possible. When such a patient needs to talk, much can be accomplished by the aide in directing the patient's thoughts toward more healthful channels.

If such methods fail, as they sometimes will, and the patient has succeeded in making a suicidal attempt, it is the aide's responsibility to remain calm and to do first things first. Before doing anything else, administer first aid. For example, if a patient is hanging he should be immediately cut down (or at least, supported until sufficient help arrives), his clothes loosened and artificial respiration begun. The same holds true for an attempted drowning. The patient must be removed from the tub, or, if he is too heavy, the water should be drained out as quickly as possible, and artificial respiration begun. If the aide is alone, he must summon help. However, the patient should *never* be left alone, since he may make a second attempt and succeed. Thus, a reliable patient can either be left with the patient or sent to the office to telephone for help.

It is a very frightening experience to come upon a person who has attempted suicide. One faces first a drastic action, and, secondly, the possibility of death. The first impulse is to run, and this frequently happens. However, running away from the emergency offers no help to an extremely needy person.

Suicides occur most often in areas infrequently used: clothes rooms, closets, private rooms, bathrooms and hallways. In terms of the time of day, suicides usually occur at the change of shifts, or early in the morning. It is easy to understand why most suicides are attempted in the early morning. A patient once described her feelings as follows:

"I used to spend a lonely, sleepless night, countlessly going over the wrongs I had done or imagined I had done. As dawn began to appear, the thought of facing another day with myself and with other people became so overwhelming that I would run and smash my head against the wall, or tear sheets, looking for *any* way out!"

As mentioned in Chapter 8, one of the major reasons for the emphasis placed on the making of rounds by personnel of both shifts at the change of shifts is to establish the safety and well-being of all patients. The high incidence of suicidal attempts made at these hours serves to add to this emphasis.

A patient who is desperate and unhappy enough to attempt to kill himself needs the friendship and the understanding of the aide more than any other patient. Such a patient attempts suicide because his inner sufferings become unbearable, or he hates himself so desperately, or he is prompted and prodded by delusions which he cannot shake. Suicide attempts are sometimes impulsive, but are more often thought about and planned. If the aide has a patient who constantly threatens and even attempts suicide and yet never succeeds, he should still not relax his vigilance. An aide tells this story:

"We had a very trying alcoholic woman who constantly talked about suicide and would grab at the ink bottles or broken glass or anything that she could get into her hands. She was always cutting herself on the wrists, splashing blood all over, and so on. I guess we got a little careless. One night I came into the deserted day room and found her hanging. She was nearly dead, and it took us a long time to revive her. Later she told me that she had thought, as she pushed the chair out from under her feet, that I was on my way to the day room. When I didn't come she became very frightened, struggled, and finally lost consciousness. She said that she had frightened herself out of the desire, and she soon got better and left the hospital. So far, she is still out. We all learned from that experience that, even though we feel that a patient is faking and will not hurt herself seriously, *accidents do happen!*"

Accidents

As frequently publicized by the National Safety Council, accidents can and do happen frequently and anywhere. In a year's time, the average family experiences any number of accidents right in the home. People slip on rugs, cut their fingers, bruise themselves in falls off chairs or ladders, take the wrong medicine, burn themselves with matches or while cooking or ironing, and choke on fish bones. All of these things may occur in the mental hospital ward, and they represent the daily emergencies with which the aide must deal.

Again, the first responsibility of the aid is prevention and foresight. For example, nurses and aides who are allowed to give medication, are always cautioned to see that the patients actually *take* the medication. In class, an aide tells of finding 25 Amytal Sodium capsules in a patient's pillow case! The patient held the pill momentarily under her tongue each night as it was administered, and as soon as possible removed it, dried it and hid it.

After a patient has broken a window every piece of glass and any sharp edges should be removed. Matches cannot be allowed in some wards because of the dangers of fire and suicide. One nurse retrieves contraband matches after each visiting day by asking patients (whom she suspects) for a light for other patients.

Old people tend to choke on their food, and the aide can avoid what could result in a fatal accident by cutting or mashing meat, celery, and the like. Old people also tend to fall easily and frequently, and fractures are very common among senile patients. Slippery rugs, inconveniently placed furniture, wet or waxed floors, and ill-fitting clothing or shoes invite such accidents.

If and when accidents do occur, they should be reported at once to the supervisor, who in turn notifies the physician. Aides should be familiar with elementary first aid and should begin giving it as soon as the accident is discovered. Every accident, no matter how unimportant it may seem at the time, and whether the accident happens to patient or employee or both, should be reported and verified in writing as soon as possible. This action serves as protection for the patient, the employee, and the institution, since many times accident reports are used as legal evidence when there is any question regarding an accident or injury.

First-aid manuals are inexpensive and easy to obtain, and each ward should have one immediately available. Such manuals list the proper remedies for various poisons, where to apply pressure when bleeding occurs, first-aid measures for burns, etc. It is unlikely that the aide or the nurse will need to do more than take the very first measures, because a physician is always available for a real emergency, even in a hospital that may be sorely understaffed.

Aides frequently have noticed and commented on the apparent lack of concern and seeming insensibility to pain which many patients display when they are ill or injured. This only serves to point up the fact that patients rarely report injuries themselves. Usually, it is another patient's word or the aide's actual discovery of symptoms that leads to care of the injury. Any untoward signs, such as increased restlessness, pallor, sweating, unaccounted-for blood, unsteady walk or unwillingness to move should be investigated, and proper steps taken to help the patient.

Physical Signs and Symptoms

One of the greatest dangers to be avoided by the aide or any other person working with persons mentally ill is failure to accept the possibility of physical as well as mental difficulty in patients. We become so concerned with the emotional problems of patients, with their emotional needs and how we can meet those needs, that we frequently overlook the very important physical problems which arise. Such problems occur frequently and oftentimes are intimately related to the emotional condition of the patient. Mind and body and the functions of each are so closely related as to create a unified whole. It stands to reason that if there is a sickness of either there is going to be a sickness of both. Mental patients who have been ill a long time exhibit certain bodily changes that are easily recognizable—changes in color and texture of the skin and the hair, changes in weight and appetite, changes, in certain conditions, of the blood vessels of the brain.

Besides the fact that the aide may be more concerned with the patient's emotional problems simply because these are the problems that are stressed for him, there are other reasons why physical problems may seem to be unimportant. For example, patients, more often than not, do not complain about their physical ailments. Or, if they do, they complain so often and so consistently that the nurse or the aide may disregard their complaints as false. There may be a tendency to feel that physical complaints are part of a "delusional system" or a bid for attention.

Actually, of course, mental patients are like everyone else and fall prey to all kinds of physical illnesses—colds, gastrointestinal upsets, broken bones, measles, intestinal obstructions and so on. *Any complaint made by a patient should be investigated and reported at once.* If a patient complains, the aide can note whether or not fever is present, whether there is a cough, bleeding, any lump or bruise, any vomiting or diarrhea or both. Since frequently patients do not actually complain, particularly those who are very sick and "out of contact," the aide can become a keen observer for anything physically out of the ordinary. It is important to note daily bowel habits; a record of weights, at least once a month, is a "must." Recently, the family of a patient who died of rapidly progressive cancer complained that the patient had not received proper care. The relatives claimed that no one had paid any attention to the patient's weight loss, lack of appetite, and frequent spells of diarrhea. At the hearing held by the hospital, the embarrassing fact was revealed that the patient's last weight had been recorded some *six months* before his death! Although blame for the patient's death was eventually canceled, that fact remained as a glaring oversight.

Some physical illnesses are not obvious, and it is well for the aide to be aware of certain behavior patterns which are not usual for the patient: for example, the active patient who suddenly wants to lie down, or to stay in bed, or becomes angry when disturbed or asked to go to a meal or to bathe; or the patient who begins rocking constantly, or holding some part of his body (rocking frequently is a symptom of pain in very young children); or a patient who seeks out a very warm spot near the radiator or asks for more cover in an already warm dormitory.

Keeping always in mind the close relationship of mind and body, and the usual signs and symptoms of physical illnesses (fever, rash, swelling, vomiting, etc.) the aide can train himself to be alert not only to the emotional needs of his patient but also to the equally important physical needs which arise so frequently among his patients.

Seizures

One of the emergencies with which the aide in the mental hospital should become familiar is how to care for the patient who has a seizure or convulsion. Seizures may occur with any type of patient (that is, acute, chronic, senile, or other) and at any time of day or night. One's first contact with a full-blown convulsion can be a rather alarming experience whether it occurs in a hospital or in the community, on a bus, the street, or other public place.

Usually, a patient who is about to have a seizure has an aura or warning—that is, he may yell, or run, or complain of a specific odor. This warning can also prepare the aide, if he is aware of it. Seizures occur in two ways: (1) as a petit mal attack—momentary loss of consciousness, sometimes with slight muscular twitch, and usually the patient does not fall; or (2) as a grand mal attack during which the patient *does* lose consciousness, falls, and the body convulses with jerking movements, lasting as long as a full minute. With a grand mal attack, involuntary urination and foaming at the mouth may occur.

The important points to remember regarding seizures are concerned with the *protection* of the patient. His fall should be broken, if possible, by a cushion, a pillow, or a coat placed under his head and the most convenient soft object available should be placed between his teeth so that he does not bite his tongue or lips or crack his teeth. Careful notation should be made of the length of the seizure, parts of the body involved, whether or not it was preceded by a warning and the general condition of the patient following the attack. Such information is very valuable to the doctor and helps him in diagnosing and treating the patient.

Patients who have seizures may present difficult behavior problems, and it is important that as stable an environment as possible be provided for them.

Feeding Problems

Feeding problems have a way of cropping up in every type of ward at some time or other. In the admitting wards, one or two patients will not eat; in the chronic services, patients sometimes eat too much and will even steal food from other patients; in the senile wards, patients cannot chew some foods or are too feeble to feed themselves; they may become constipated and ill and do not want to eat; in the medical-surgical wards patients cannot or will not eat certain foods, or certain foods will give a number of patients diarrhea. Patients in any of these types of wards may have emotional blocks about eating: they may feel that the food is poisoned, that they are unworthy of eating it, that they can starve themselves to death, or that their religion prevents them from eating.

All of these feeding problems are serious and must be attended to by nursing personnel. Occasionally, it is necessary to seek medical help (i.e., the use of medication before meals or the use of some other specific treatment). Tube feeding, a method commonly used in the past, does more harm than good, and should be used only as a *very last resort*.

The first thing which the aide must determine is the *reason why his patient will not eat*. Once he establishes the reason, he can proceed with one of several plans. For example, a patient may dislike eating with other patients, or, to be more exact, eating in front of anyone. If this is true, he can be fed by himself until such time as he feels that once again he can eat with his group. One of the aides in a chronic ward had worked endlessly with a patient who would not sleep or move or eat. She had to be forced into all of the necessary activities of daily life. Among other things, she would not talk, so the reasons for her behavior were not known. On this particular ward, aides served trays from a hot cart in the ward kitchen. One day the aide accidentally left a full tray on the serving cart while she carried two others to patients in the ward. The above-mentioned patient who was standing just outside the kitchen door, darted in and consumed the whole meal that had been left on the table. From that time on, the aide "accidentally" left the full tray each meal, and eventually the patient was able to accept a tray in the day room with other patients.

If a patient feels, because of his particular religious beliefs, that he cannot eat, sometimes it is helpful to ask the assistance of the chaplain of his particular religion. Or, it is sometimes permissible to allow the patient's family to bring in to him specially prepared foods which he can accept and which he *will* eat.

Other and more commonplace methods of handling feeding problems include the serving of smaller portions to patients, the determination of a patient's favorite foods and the obtaining of same, the use of spoon feeding until the patient is able or willing to feed himself. Occasionally, it is important for the aide to eat with his patient, or, at least, he can taste some of the food to "prove" to the patient that it is not poisoned.

Patience and meticulous attention to detail are very important with feeding problems. This is often very difficult when the aide is alone and has many patients to look after, but the results can be very gratifying when a stubborn feeding problem has at last been conquered.

Fear—Yours and the Patient's

As has been mentioned previously, fear is one of the most devastating factors present in mental illness. The patient is afraid of the hospital and the people in it, he is afraid of what will happen to him—what will be done to him, he is afraid of the dark and of other patients, his delusions may make him afraid of what will "get him," of "who is after him"; he is afraid of the things he sees and hears and feels through his hallucinations.

All of these fears create special problems and emergencies, because they cause the patient to act impulsively, or to behave in an aggressive and angry manner. For example, fear may impel him to try suicide or to break out windows in an attempt to "get away"; it may cause him to be mischievous and even malicious, i.e., spitting at people (aides say this behavior makes them angrier than any other one thing patients may do); fear may cause patients to attack other patients or personnel. In each case, the need is for security and friendship. The aide, in his close relationship with patients, can offer both. *But* not if he is afraid himself!

Patients easily sense fear in another person and are quick to capitalize on it. There is no doubt that there are times when even the most experienced aide is afraid and rightfully so. A little healthy fear helps to fortify one's alertness and observation. But the kind of fear that paralyzes one's good judgment should be eliminated quickly.

Elimination of fear usually comes through two channels: First, if an orientation program is offered, strict attention can be given it, since it is through knowledge of patients and their behavior that nursing the mentally ill loses its "unknown" quality. Secondly, if the aide is fortunate, he will work, at least at first, with older, more experienced aides, and from them he learns to use his most valuable tools—his innate feelings for people less fortunate than he, and the utilization of his own past experiences and the consequently acquired *common sense.*

After a sufficient length of time, one comes to realize that patients are, after all, just people who are mixed up and need help in getting themselves straightened out. The fear of physical harm becomes lessened with experience, since a patient will seldom, if ever, attack an aide unless provoked. A little kindness, patience, even firmness go a long way. And it is well to remember that some patients make trusted friends and will help out in many a difficult situation.

Religious Problems

It has been said that there is no such thing as an atheist, since by denying a superior Being, we admit the existence of one. Albeit, nearly *everyone* has religious feeling and belief, and most of us accept a formalized religion. The aide must be tolerant of his patient's beliefs, regardless of whether or not such beliefs agree with his own religious convictions. Religion is one of the strongest influences in human life, and mental patients in common with all other people have certain religious needs which must be met. Religious feeling is a very personal matter with most people, and in many instances it can initiate emotionally charged situations. The aide may get into real difficulty if he attempts to discuss religious problems with his patients, and he is only justified in maintaining, openly, the philosophy that life is worth living and that there are consoling reasons for the problems of life. Above and beyond this simple philosophy, the aide can only request the aid of the hospital chaplain or the family pastor. Either should be summoned as often as necessary, although the physician's guidance should always be asked, since occasionally the patient's need to see his pastor is exaggerated and can become extremely trying to all concerned. Suicidal patients frequently respond very well to talks with the pastor of their own faith.

It goes without saying that the chaplain should be called immediately for a dying patient. The aide should be ready to give any and all assistance to the chaplain at this time.

The aide can be very instrumental in stimulating interest in his patients to attend church services. Most hospitals offer services for all three major faiths, and in some areas, patients are escorted to town for services. The aide can inform his patients of such services and can make sure that patients are clean and dressed in time to go.

The aide who attends church services, religious singing groups, and religious social functions with patients should be prepared for any emergencies that may disturb the occasions. A patient may have a seizure or may become so loud or active that he disturbs others. In either case, the aide can care for his patient and remove him to his ward as soon as possible.

Careful observation of religious activity and the reporting or recording of such activity by the aide can be extremely helpful to the doctor, the chaplain, and the patient's family.

Away Without Leave

Mental hospital personnel must, of necessity, be much concerned with patients who leave the ward or the grounds without permission. There are many good reasons for this. Some patients may escape with the express intent of committing suicide. If the patient is a known suicidal risk every means should be immediately employed to find him. Some patients are dangerous to the community, and particularly to their relatives. Proper notification of family and police is essential in this case. Some patients are "cranks" and head for the home of the nearest Government official or other important person, and there they may create a commotion. Still other patients, particularly women, may get into difficulty with promiscuous persons who have no regard for the mental limitations of their illness. Finally, there are patients, especially old people, who wander off in their confusion and may become lost for a sufficient length of time to die from exposure.

The importance of the aide's knowing the whereabouts and the activity of each of his patients cannot be stressed enough. Sometimes, it is essential to count patients, as, for example, when taking large groups to meals, or to a social function. Such counting cannot be done by yelling names and expecting an answer. Each patient should not be checked off until seen and *known* by the aide responsible for him.

Patients leave the hospital by various ways and means. Most often they await an opportunity and slip through a door unnoticed. Frequently, if they are intent upon escape, they will badger any new employee to let them out. Many a new aide has had the experience of being told by a patient that the patient is "allowed out" or "has privileges," only to find later that he has released a real risk. It is better for the aide to endure a little embarrassment over being "new" than to allow a patient who is unknown to him to leave the ward.

Patients are quite clever at fashioning makeshift keys from tableware, coat hangers, etc. It should not be necessary to count tableware, but careful observation of patients after meals will usually reveal any restricted articles.

Patients should be taken outside at every opportunity. If patients are known as "escape risks" they can still be allowed outside with the group, if there is a sufficient number of accompanying personnel—certainly *at least* two aides or nurses. If a patient then leaves the group, one person can stay with the group while the other goes for help in retrieving the patient.

One of the factors overlooked in the matter of patients who are returned from being "away without leave" is the patient's own feeling about the entire event. Too often those persons receiving the patient make sarcastic remarks or goad the patient with questions concerning his absence, or may even punish the patient. The patient may feel embarrassed about the incident or may be frustrated and angry over it. A better procedure would be to treat him as a readmission without discussion of his escape and with the same kindness and respect.

Finally, in the event of discovering a patient away without leave, the aide should immediately notify his supervisor and begin a thorough search of the surrounding area. Most hospitals require a written report, and such a report usually must contain several points of information which only the responsible aide can give: i.e., what the patient was wearing, when last seen and by whom, and is the escape device known?

Escapes are not as frequent as the public might assume, especially considering the several means at the patient's disposal. The alert and conscientious aide is largely responsible for this fact.

Introduction

As he began to look ahead toward his own future, he recognized that significant changes were taking place in the entire program of prevention and care in mental illness. As he observed the powerful influence of more help and new drugs, he became aware that his own role would soon change. He was pleased because he realized that some of the arduous routine of his job would disappear, and he would have many more opportunities to relate to his patients— to get to know them as individuals. He knew, too, that some of his feelings of optimism regarding mental patients would become realistic— that there would be more unlocked doors, more organized rehabilitation programs, and more of his patients leaving the hospital.

——————————10

Your Role in
Newer Developments

In view of the changing concepts in nursing care of the
mentally ill, probably no part of this book should be studied
more carefully than this chapter.

Many of the hospitalized mental patients in the present
optimistic psychiatric era are people who can *manage* themselves. They can control their "acting out"; they can (and
want to) take care of their own personal hygiene and dress;
and they can estimate and fulfill their own needs for rest and
nourishment. The resident hospital population continues to
decline, as it has for some 15 years. To those who have worked
for 15 years (or more) in mental hospitals, these things represent a dramatic change. For example, the courses being
given to the psychiatric aide today are for more concerned
with the *intangibles* involved in caring for the mentally ill
(communication skills, the dynamics of human relationships)
than they were 15 or 20 years ago. Lesson plans at that time
were developed around such matters as: "How to Approach
the Violent Patient," "How to Apply Restraints," and "How
to Assist the Doctor with a Tube-feeding." In the average
mental hospital of today, the aide would be unlikely to face
any of these three problems (or similar ones) even once in
the course of a year!

The fact that the tranquilizing drugs have helped to bring about this "dramatic change" has already been noted. *Equally important*, but far less publicly acclaimed, has been the effect of improved legislative awareness and the consequent increase in financial appropriations for the care of mental patients. These appropriations have made possible the following positive gains: the procurement of better qualified personnel at all levels, the restablishment of comprehensive and adequate educational programs—particularly for aides—and the development of more realistic salary scales which have appreciably reduced personnel turnover. As will be discussed in Chapter 11, the emergence of community mental health centers has also created change in the number of people admitted to mental hospitals.

What does all this mean for the psychiatric aide? No one will deny that it is *still* the aide who consistently spends the greatest amount of time with patients, because aides still outnumber, by far, all other types of personnel caring for the 1,600,000 mentally ill in this country.

The role of the psychiatric aide is changing as newer concepts emerge. He is no longer a "custodian" who, in addition, attends to the patient's physical needs. Although he continues to help the patient with the latter, he now assumes the role of the compassionate and reassuring companion, aware of the elementary dynamics of human behavior and relationships and skilled in the basic principles of communication.

Some Emerging Special Groups

Among the vast numbers of people in our mental hospitals, two kinds of patients in particular are receiving more and more attention. These are the patients with so-called "special privileges" and convalescent patients. The new emphasis on these two groups is justified indeed, since they are fast becoming the largest number of patients. Of course, they do represent divergent problems, and thus they will be discussed under their individual headings.

Patients with Special Privileges

The term "privileged patient" can mean a number of things, but in general it means a patient who has recovered sufficiently to assume varying degrees of responsibility—from "off-ward privileges" to living and working in the community or in a foster home or "halfway house." It could also conceivably refer to the many patients who are being treated in a day or night hospital.

Convalescent Patients

One often overhears aides say, "I don't like working on a convalescent ward. That's a lazy man's job. There's nothing to do!" This, of course, is not true. *Any job is what you make of it.* Working on an "open," or convalescent, ward can be easy in one sense. There are not the exacting, demanding duties involved in other words—that is, disturbed, senile, medical-surgical, or admitting wards. On such wards as these, there is always physical work to be done—beds to be made, patients to be showered and fed, active patients seeking attention, errands to run, various therapies in progress, and so on. The convalescent patient has reached a point where he can care for his own basic needs and is on the last lap of his journey back into the community. What possible problems can the aide have in such a situation? He has "good" patients who help him keep his ward immaculate; many of his patients are out all day working in industrial therapy or various other forms of occupational therapy; almost all of his patients will make and keep their own appointments with doctors and other helpers.

It is on the convalescent ward that the aide needs to capitalize on his *awareness*, his perceptiveness and mental abilities. In other kinds of wards, needs are obvious—the problem is

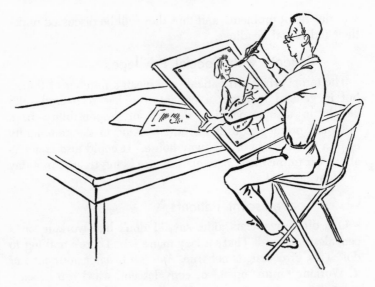

Convalescent

right there, it faces one, and it must be solved. Patients who are convalescent offer three major problems the aide must cope with. One is the need to provide constant impetus and motivation for the patient to continue his healthful trend. In other words, it is important that the patient be provided with maximum activity, both in work and play, for most of his waking hours. Secondly, the aide always should be on the lookout for any tendency on the part of his patients to fall back. A patient who gets up late, misses a day or two of work, becomes withdrawn from the rest of the group, seems to be *afraid* on visiting day ("I shall soon have to face these people every single day. I couldn't do it before—can I do it now?") or complains of various physical ailments, is one who may be slipping. He will need concentrated support, sincere interest in his projects, honest friendship. The third problem is that of suicide. It is a known fact that suicides occur more frequently as a patient is *apparently getting better* than in very sick wards. Remember that when patients are recovering, particularly from depressions, there is not only the impulse toward suicide but also the necessary activity has been generated. In deep depression there is not usually the energy to go through with the act, even though the desire may be there. (The problem of suicide is included in Chapter 9 and has been discussed more thoroughly there.)

Accurate observation of patients and their various activities is essential on the open ward. This is a form of prevention, just as it is practiced in the community. When the patient demonstrates unusual behavior of any kind or to any degree, it should be reported immediately to a responsible person (supervisor or doctor) so that appropriate steps may be taken to eliminate the possibilities of the patient's becoming very sick again.

It is particularly important that the aide working in the convalescent ward avoid getting a feeling of uselessness. His job is very important, because he is the one who encourages his patient to work, who makes it easier by stimulating an attitude of hopefulness for his patient to face a community which unfortunately is not often healthfully educated to mental illness, who helps his patient to develop the technics of productive interpersonal relationships and recognizes and takes steps to minimize his patients' natural fears about "beginning life all over again."

The "Open Door Policy"

In the past 10 years, this country has begun to catch up with England in terms of "open" wards. In one English hospital there are no locked doors, and all patients can come and go as they please, although most are restricted to "within the hospital grounds." Reports from hospitals in the United States now indicate that allowing patients to come and go, in and out, as they please during the daylight hours has *not* created any increase in the number of A.W.O.L. patients. Patients are allowed the freedom of the hospital grounds, many can go "up street," and some go back and forth to regular activities or jobs every day.

For the psychiatric aide, open wards reemphasize his responsibility for careful *observation and the prompt reporting* of anything unusual about his patients. (Some patients who have been given Thorazine may obtain, in a very short time, a severe sunburn, unless they are properly cautioned before they leave the ward.) In addition, it means the development of an ever-increasing *awareness*. This is particularly true for the aide who is with his patients during the evening hours. If the patients are out of the ward most of the time on most days, they are observed much less frequently by the nurse and the doctor. During the evening, as patients return from their various daily activities, the aide should spend much time circulating among them and talking things over. In this way, he can perceive when a patient is not healthfully assimilating his new freedom, when a patient seems to be relapsing and needs more attention and perhaps a temporary return to a more secure environment, when a patient has some physical problem which needs to be evaluated, and how certain patients are responding to prescribed therapies (occupational, recreational and industrial) or to job assignments outside of the hospital. The occasional "patient romance," although it may be healthful, should be known to each of the patient's doctors.

Rehabilitation Houses

In the early 1960's, one of the most promising of the "newer developments" was the establishment in nearby communities of Rehabilitation Houses for discharged mental patients (called in some areas, "Halfway Houses"). These houses provided a distinctly valuable supplement for some hospitals which have had inadequate (and often nontherapeutic) "Foster Home" programs.

The house itself, unless newly built for the purpose, is usually a residence in town which is large, cheerful and homelike. It is purchased by the state or other sponsoring agency, and "house-parents" are employed to manage the house and to assist the discharged patients (with the help of the hospital rehabilitation "team"—usually doctor, nurse and social worker) in their adjustment to community life. Frequently, the house-parents are selected from among the more experienced aides at the hospital—usually an older, married couple. They, of course, live right at the house and manage its affairs as anyone would do in a large family home. Patients, as part of their program, assist with housework, cooking, cleaning and laundry. The main purpose of the Rehabilitation House is to bridge the gap between the mental hospital and the community—particularly in those patients with no families or patients for whom return to their own family environment would be inadvisable.

As soon as they are acclimated to the house (living *away* from the hospital, which for some may be the first real visit to the "outside" world for 15 or 20 years), they are encouraged to become acclimated to the community. Ultimate goal for these patients is their procurement of a job within the community which will be not only a satisfying job but one which eventually will allow them to be self-supporting and thus able to find and manage their own living quarters. Besides the guidance and the reassurance of the house-parents, these patients are visited frequently and given counseling by vocational rehabilitation personnel—people who are specifically prepared to help patients with job placement and to analyze with the patient, his individual capacity for various types of work.

Perhaps, one of the most valuable outcomes of this particular type of rehabilitation program has been *community acceptance of the discharged mental patient*. It has not always been easy to gain such acceptance. However, once gained, it spreads through the community—from those residents who live on the same street as the Rehabilitation House and its members to the prospective employers who in many instances have co-operated to the fullest extent in helping the patient through participation in the joint hospital-community project. Obviously, as more community mental health centers are developed, there should be less need for halfway houses.

Foster Homes and Patient "Friends"

Even as we begin the 1970's, the Foster Home program has not, as yet, been completely successful. There are several reasons for this: (1) difficulty in selecting "therapeutic" homes. Since most individuals or families who take patients into their home get paid for it, such responsibility can easily fall into the hands of unscrupulous persons whose first interest definitely does not lie with the patient. (2) Many people are reluctant to take people into their homes who have once been "crazy." (3) It is difficult to give foster homes proper guidance and supervision in many short-staffed hospitals. Witnessing what has gone on in the famed colony of Gheel, Belgium, for about 400 years, there is no question that, under the proper circumstances, the foster home can be a valuable asset in patient rehabilitation.

In a few communities in the United States, broad-minded community members have became patient "friends." That is, they have "adopted" a patient (who has no known relatives or friends outside of the hospital), taking the patient into their homes for a day or a weekend or a 2-week vacation and remembering him on his birthday or special holidays. This practice, too, has its beneficial effect on community-mental hospital relations.

Remotivation

Remotivation* is a planned group meeting in which a sharing or pooling of ideas about everyday things promotes personal interaction between aide and patients and among patients themselves. Probably, the success of this simple group interaction is due to the fact that it reminds the patient of the *real world* in which he has lived—work, play, current events —and is an attempt to make that real world more desirable than his sick world.

Because of the ataractic drugs, improved facilities and better qualified personnel, patients have become more accessible for pyschotherapy and more responsive to nursing and aide care, but there are still numbers of patients who get little or no treatment. Remotivation enables the aide to reach his patients in a helpful way, over and above the daily custodial care which previously has constituted the somewhat limited role of the psychiatric aide.

Remotivation is not psychotherapy as such. Instead, it is a method of aide-patient interaction which increases and strengthens the mutual contact. It is a method which can become an accepted, hospital-wide program, available to any and all *interested* aides and adaptable in any ward in the average mental hospital, particularly large public mental hospitals.

The *interest of the aide, mentioned above,* is probably the single, most important qualification necessary for the aide's successful participation in a remotivation program. Other important qualifications would include: a warm and under-

---

* Information in this section was excerpted from a manual on remotivation written by the author (see reading list).

standing attitude toward patients, resourcefulness, the development of comfort in speaking before a group and the willingness to go further in the job than "just what is necessary."

Along with all that the psychiatric aide can give to a program in remotivation, the program can also give something to the aide. It increases his contact with his patients in such a way that it is not just part of the ordinary, everyday routine. However, the aide should keep in mind that he is not *teaching* patients, although it is true that both the patient and the aide do learn from these sessions. These are not *classes*. They are group meetings in which a sharing or pooling of ideas about everyday things promotes personal interaction between aide and patients and among patients themselves.

In its original form, remotivation is based on 5 steps. In practice, it has been demonstrated that adherence to these five steps creates more stable and lasting programs. For the psychiatric aide, full knowledge and appreciation of these steps provides him with a starting point, a level of continuity, and a hopeful and promising conclusion.

Remotivation has been extensively developed and utilized since it was originally evolved in 1956. Its outstanding merits include the following points: (1) it can be used successfully with almost any type of mental patients; (2) the aide-leaders are not required to possess any highly specialized qualifications in order to participate in the program; (3) the program reaches many patients who otherwise might participate in only the most meager of hospital routines; and (4) it changes the role concept of the psychiatric aide from that of "custodian" to that of a valuable and contributing member of the mental hospital team.

Day and Night Hospitals

Within the last 10 years or so, a number of mental hospital facilities have set aside certain wards as "day" or "night hospitals." Patients who belong to the day hospital report for a designated time during each day, but return to their homes and families at night. Most of the day programs include group or individual psychotherapy, occupational and recreational therapy, vocational training, and so on. Of course, the night hospital is just the opposite. The patient carries on his usual job or home tasks during the day but comes into the hospital in the evening for the same kind of program, and then sleeps there. For some people this avoids the necessity for complete hospitalization.

The role of the psychiatric aide—and of course, psychiatric aides comprise a good part of the personnel in day and night hospitals—is essentially the same as his role on a convalescent ward. He is expected to participate in various patient activities, to be a good listener and to provide the kind of stable, uninvolved friendships the patient has missed in the community from which he came.

Psychiatric Units in General Hospitals

Again, the same kinds of responsibilities are assumed by aides in the psychiatric units of general hospitals. Usually, these are small, intensified-treatment areas in which the aide deals less with large groups of patients and more with individuals or small groups and where he assumes a more specific role as a member of the psychiatric team.

One out of every 10 of the 1,300 general hospitals admit psychiatric patients, but it is still questionable whether these units have achieved one of their main objectives—that of removing the stigma of "mental hospital" from the patient. Too often, these units are still segregated from the rest of the hospital, not only geographically but also by virtue of the attitude of the staff. Other patients still ask, fearfully: "Where's that nut ward?" Aides who work in such wards can help to alleviate this problem by maintaining open and communicative relationships with other staff members and patients.

Introduction

One of his coworkers came in early one morning and talked to him about a new job he would be going to in a few weeks. He was going to be a "community mental health aide" in a new community mental health center that had opened up in a nearby town. The coworker was a tall, good-natured black man who spoke fluent Spanish, and who had been well liked by the patients in his ward.

He seemed very enthusiastic about his new role, describing it as "helping the people I've lived around all my life" to keep out of a mental hospital. "They need somebody who can understand their problems—their way of life. And, frankly, the professionals, for the most part, can't understand. I know what it's all about. I grew up in all of it."

—————————————————————————11

Community Mental
Health Centers

In the field of psychiatry and mental health, the 1960's will be remembered as the decade in which the first real efforts were made to concentrate on moving into the community to reach troubled people before they needed hospitalization and to support former patients who had returned to the community after having been hospitalized for mental illness.

Dealing with emotionally disturbed people in the community—sometimes effectively and sometimes not—has gone on for centuries. Gheel has been mentioned in the previous chapter, as have foster homes and rehabilitation, or "'halfway," houses. The community mental health center is an entity in itself and, during the 1960's, had a rather difficult time getting off the ground. At first, these centers for the most part were staffed by psychiatrists, psychologists, and social workers. Only recently have psychiatric nurses joined the team, and even more recently, aides—particularly in the inner-city ghetto areas—have been included in these centers.

For a number of years there have been specialized community centers, many of them organized and operated under private auspices. They include centers for the mentally retarded, for disturbed children, and guidance and marriage clinics for adults. The community mental health center is designed so that it does not have the limitations these previously mentioned efforts have had and still have.

Community Mental Health Centers

The community mental health center is usually expected to serve populations of up to 200,000 people. It should provide a variety of services, and it should be easily available to the community it purports to serve. Its main objective should be the prevention of serious mental illness so that hospitalization would not be required; it also should promote good mental health, and be a treatment center for people who are having their first bout with mental illness or who have already had episodes of illness and need support and counsel to continue a recuperative process; and finally, it should provide around-the-clock emergency service to provide crisis intervention. A specific example of the latter type of community service is the suicide prevention center, which provides, at the least, a 24-hour telephone answering service for anyone who wishes to talk to someone about his suicidal tendencies.

The role of the aide in such a center, although it has hardly begun to develop, seems very vital, particularly in ghetto areas where the population is often made up of foreign-born residents who may not even speak English. Aides drawn from this very population can work effectively with members of their own ethnic group in terms of cultural, temperamental, and linguistic understanding.

In talking with persons deeply involved in making these centers work, one hears accounts of how aides, recruited from the neighborhood and trained "on-the-job," have convinced troubled families to come to the center; talked friends or neighbors out of suicidal attempts; persuaded pregnant women not to try aborting themselves; and have been able to explain a treatment regimen like regular medication—in the community member's terms. An example comes to mind: A nurse told a ghetto resident to take his medication "after meals." The patient ate frequently and irregularly or hardly at all. The aide, overhearing the instructions, suggested that the patient be told to take his medication when he got up, at noon, and in the early evening.

Although there are some differences in the populations of—and thus the therapeutic approach to—large urban-community mental health centers and those serving rural populations, the need is as great for the one as for the other. And there is a similar need for qualified staff. Authorities predict a tremendous growth in the number of these centers throughout the United States in the immediate future, providing that means can be found to finance them. As of July, 1969, federal grants totaling $292.2 million have been awarded for the construction and staffing of 376 centers. It is projected that by 1980, 2,000 community mental health centers will have been funded.*

The movement is not without problems. In the community health center concept there is some danger that more has been promised than can be delivered. Money at the local level is scarce, and the original funding law assumed that financial responsibility would be taken over locally. Some critics feel it is a "watered-down" program of psychiatry; some ghetto residents are suspicious that the movement is intended to "simmer them down" and help them accept the intolerable conditions under which they live. But the program's proponents are convinced that it offers some new answers to some very old problems and that it helps people develop and use their inner strengths to begin attacking the problems that are part of their daily lives.

Obviously, there is a new and challenging role opening up for psychiatric aides in these centers—both urban and rural—and there will be a need for personnel of all kinds. The citizens in communities presently being served by these centers have begun to assume an active voice about what services are

*Facts About Mental Illness (1969 Fact Sheet), National Association for Mental Health, 10 Columbus Circle, New York, N.Y. 10019.

needed and some of the ways in which these services can be implemented.

Until specific educational programs in community mental health become more available to prospective aides, it would seem advisable for those interested in working in such centers to gain valuable experience beforehand in a psychiatric hospital or unit.

Regardless of where he seeks help—hospital, clinic, emergency room, or community mental health center—the emotionally distraught person still needs wise understanding and the knowledge that those who reach out to help him recognize that he is an individual and his bewilderment is not his alone.

Introduction

He would be fifty before long—and fifty isn't really very far from seventy. He wondered what he would be like (and who would be caring for him if he needed care). Would he be ill and feeble? Would he be in good physical condition but not thinking very straight? Would he have known loss and grief?

Occasionally he was called on to help out on the geriatric wards—men's and women's. He wanted always to be kind and gentle with these people, but sometimes they could really aggravate him! But many of them had been important people—and all of them had been important to someone. He teased them and coaxed them, helped them to be clean and comfortable, and, most of all, he tried to help them while away the long hours with some measure of pleasure.

—————————————————12

Older Patients

Anyone who has worked for any length of time in a large mental hospital knows that one of the chief problems encountered is care of the aged. We are becoming increasingly aware of this problem as it continues to grow. Our population figures indicate that the greatest number in our population are those over 60 years of age, and yet the facilities for caring for these older people are minimal. Many of the older people in mental hospitals today are there simply because there is no other place to care for them, or their families either do not want or are not able to keep them at home.

One of the greatest incentives for the giving of kind and good care to old people is the realization that we, ourselves, will be old someday. It is difficult to imagine how we will feel, since it is an experience not yet known. However, of one thing we are certain: it is at this time in life that we will most need friends—someone to love us and to care what happens to us. Our progress, and we know this well, leads only toward death, and we need to face it with calmness and spiritual dignity.

The old people in mental hospitals are usually grouped into two major types of illness: (1) those with cerebral arteriosclerosis (hardening of the blood vessels of the brain, causing changes in emotional and physiologic behavior) and (2) those

Older Patients

with senile psychosis (an organic degeneration of the brain in which there is an exaggeration of the normal changes of old age). These two illnesses account for a large percentage of new admissions, usually over the age of 60, but because of the high incidence of death among these patients, they comprise only about 18 per cent of the total hospital population.

As the aide watches the old patients placed in his care, he will notice the peculiarities of behavior that make it necessary for them to be hospitalized. Old people are irritable, forgetful, sometimes childishly playful; they collect things, may be depressed, may misidentify people, become suspicious and have feelings of being persecuted. Old people have many physiologic problems. They need to be fed frequently, in small amounts, and cannot eat all kinds of food; they need to be kept warm and dry; their skin needs special care, and their elimination is often faulty. There is always the danger of a serious physical illness; for instance, they develop pneumonia quickly when not allowed to exercise, and they are subject to severe circulatory disturbances (heart failure, stroke).

Mostly, they are likeable, amusing and fairly easily satisfied. Old people are very lonely, appreciate little things, center their lives around past events, love companionship and for the most part respond both to the vitality of youth and the warmth of being mothered.

Next to the care of infirmary patients, old patients need the most attention in relation to their physical care. Specific problems should be pointed out, and some solutions offered. Feeding is one of these problems. This kind of patient should be allowed extra time for eating, and food should be hot, easily digestible and soft. The aide should notice whether or not patients have difficulty in cutting food; if necessary, he should offer assistance. The patient should be as comfortable as possible while eating. For example, if his food is served on a tray in the ward day room, some provision should be made so that he does not have to hold the tray on his lap. Balance is hard for him. Should he drop the tray he would become very embarrassed, for he is already aware of his lessening abilities, and he dislikes having others aware of them. It is also important that old people have some kind of snack before going to bed—warm milk or bread and butter. This will help them to sleep better.

Bathing old people involves certain hazards. One of the most tragic of these is improper water temperature. Patients have been severely and even fatally burned because an aide or a nurse left them alone in a bath and did not test the water before placing them in the tub. *Do not depend on regulators or even bath thermometers!* The time-honored method of placing the wrist in the bath water *first* is the only sure way. Old people should not have to take shower baths, since they are often unsteady and may slip and fall. When giving an old person a tub bath, stay with him. If he has to be bathed, gentleness and thoroughness are important, as skin is soft, thin and in need of good care. Cleanliness is very important to anyone's well-being. With the aged, it is particularly important, because the skin breaks down easily, forming bedsores, rashes or ulcers.

Old people tend to become constipated easily, and often, because of their forgetfulness, their "busyness" or their feebleness, they will not be conscious of it themselves. Constipation in the aged may result in serious impaction and intestinal obstruction that necessitates surgery. The aide should watch for signs of constipation in all of his old patients—bad breath, a puffy abdomen, loss of appetite, nausea, or straining at toilet. Any such signs should be reported to the doctor so that the necessary relief can be given. Similarly, diarrhea, fairly common among old people, particularly in the hot summer months, should be reported as soon as noted. A severe bout of diarrhea can so exhaust and deplete an old person that he may die.

Old people will have to urinate more often and may have to get up once or twice during the night. Frequent toileting of the older patient eliminates soiling (which, again, is embarrassing for him), and the danger of slipping on the wet floor in his hurry to get to the bathroom. Many old people wet the bed at night, and changes should be made as soon as the wet bed is noticed. Many senile units schedule routine changes during the night, but patients' beds should still be checked between times. The old patient feels particularly lost and alone at night, and when he is cold and wet it must increase this feeling a hundredfold.

One final major problem in the physical care realm is that of falls or accidents. Old people are usually unsteady on their feet. Obstructions should be removed from their usual paths (to the bathroom, the dining room, the day room, or the porch), and the friendly, comforting arm of the aide or the nurse should be offered whenever possible. Low beds are recommended for old patients, and if a high bed must be used, it should be against a wall or provided with sideboards. If a patient falls or is pushed or struck by another patient, he should always be seen by the doctor as soon as possible. Injuries are not always obvious, and fractures are common.

Much emphasis has been placed on physical care in the foregoing paragraphs. Because of the overcrowded conditions and the shortage of personnel which exist in the senile wards of most large mental hospitals, this basic care is often all that can be offered. However, older patients have emotional needs, too. As mentioned before, they are lonely and crave companionship, particularly with people their own age. A group sitting in the sun, chatting and reminiscing about the past can be a very contented group, just as we see them in city parks or in the country, sewing or canning or sitting around someone's yard. They look forward to visitors as eagerly as any other patient. They like simple activities as, for instance, chess, checkers and cards for the old men, or sewing and reading for the old ladies. Older patients are afraid to be left alone, and even if left with only one other person to whom they can talk, can be quite content. At times, they become very irritable or excited, which is not good for them, since it may bring on exhaustion or a stroke. Aides should not address old people by familiar nicknames such as "Pop" or "Granny." Many of them are well aware that they are in an institution, and this loss of dignity is hard enough to bear without having those who care for them add to the indignity. Church services are very important to most older patients, especially those who are aware that they will soon have to face death.

The aide should learn to be particularly patient about the older person's forgetfulness. Many, many times he will have to repeat his name or repeat instructions to his elderly patients. With this type of patient, memory for past events is usually quite good, but memory of recent events (even what he has just eaten for lunch!) is remarkably poor. It embarrasses him to be asked questions when he cannot remember, and he will likely become either irritated and cranky about it, or he will make up some suitable answer. Old people may have some harmless little habits which should be indulged. For example, a little old lady comes to the nurse's station every day and gets her hat and pocketbook. "Dressing up" with these two items, she carefully tries all the doors in the ward, and then, failing to get out, "visits" little groups of cronies about the patients' living room.

Old people, like all other patients, need to be understood and loved. If their physical wants are taken care of, if they have companions and light activities, and if they know that someone cares about them, they can while away their hours in comparative peace. Television has been a blessing in the geriatric wards. It is surprising that even the very old respond to this diversion. The six wards of the geriatric service of a nearby mental hospital have to share a portable television set. Each ward keeps it for two weeks, which means that each ward has television only once every three months! Some of the old people cry when it must be moved to the next ward. The aides find their work easier, and certainly more pleasant when their patients are quiet and interested rather than when they are crying, calling frequently for bedpans, or wriggling around precariously in their chairs. Even a small radio does much to take away an air of loneliness. Old men like to watch or listen to sports programs; listening to music or watching dancing seems to please the older women.

One indulgent aide who is responsible for many old men through the night hours has two elderly gentlemen who are very noisy when put to bed. Each night he moves their beds into the patients' living area and places them in front of the television set. There they remain contentedly quiet, watching the programs, until they fall asleep and can be gently moved back to the sleeping quarters.

Most of all, old people want company. It is rather sad that there are not more visitors who come to the geriatric wards to see patients. Visitors who can sit with patients, bring them something tasty to eat and, especially, bring them news from home, are an important part of that patient's meager life.

Introduction

In his earlier days on the admitting ward, he had noticed that there seemed to be more and more admissions of young people. They were not necessarily addicts or "hippies"; there were many who were seriously disturbed children and young adults. They often seemed lost in the adult patient world; occasionally, however, an older patient or aide would offer the kind of mature support they needed.

After a while the hospital opened a children's unit and then an adolescents' unit. A school program was begun and the youngsters responded well.

There were problems—harassment of the aides, smuggling in of drugs, some destructive behavior. But the aides who worked with young people were knowledgeable and very patient people. And they became important friends to their youthful charges.

Younger Patients

Certainly, in the present decade, the troubled adolescents in our society will be a segment of the disturbed community that psychiatric hospitals and community mental health centers will have to learn to deal with. There are still many unanswered questions revolving around how to help an increasing population of disturbed young people.

Caring for younger patients is a relatively new area of concern in mental hospitals. Prior to World War II, most of the teen-age (or younger) patients in mental hospitals were mentally retarded and not necessarily mentally disturbed. The first residential facilities for adolescents did not come into being until the 1940's, and a real increase in adolescent admissions did not begin until the late 1950's. In fact, one of the major reasons for frustration in attempts to help this group is the fact that most of our facilities were built and staffed to serve adult patients. At the present time, the adolescent is present in larger and larger numbers in the hospital census.

To quote a few statistics (from the National Association for Mental Health, Inc.) 10 per cent of all school-age children have emotional problems requiring psychiatric help. The number of young people aged 15 to 24 in mental hospitals has risen 35 per cent, and an additional increase of 70 per cent is predicted for the year 1970. Latest figures (1967) show that 12,610 children under 18 years of age were admitted to public mental hospitals for the first hospitalization for serious mental disorder. In the same year, about 465,000 children were served in psychiatric clinics.

Basically, adolescence means growing up. It covers a rather wide period from puberty (about 12 years of age) until the late teens or early twenties. But the age of adolescence is, in a sense, expanding, and can be divided into three more specific periods—from 12 to 14, 15 to 17, and 17 to beginning of adulthood. Behavior can be quite different during these three periods. One often hears remarks like the following: "When I was 12 and my brother 16, we might as well have been strangers. But when he was 24 and I was 20, we were great friends and more often than not socialized together."

Young people today are "more to be pitied than censured." They are growing up in a world that is very difficult for the wisest adult to understand—if, indeed, even *he* can. Everywhere the youngster looks, his security is menaced—by threatened cataclysms of war (not to mention nuclear holocaust), civil disorder, antiquated education systems, and his adult role-models who drink, smoke, take pills, and themselves falter in insecurity.

His reaction to this and the technological revolution of the past half-century, a revolution that has accelerated man far past his human ability to cope with it, has been a growing attitude of disdain for and independence from adult influence. The result, commonly known as the "generation gap," is very real as the adult recoils from young people's "way-out" hair and dress styles, what he views as their promiscuous sexual behavior, their seeming indifference toward assuming responsibility in the work world, and an alarming tendency on the part of young people to be attracted to drugs. At the same time, youth views the "over 30's" as stuffy, bigoted, politically naive, and unduly conservative.

Patterns of Treatment

There is still much speculation as to how to help the adolescent who is disturbed enough to be hospitalized, but some concepts deserve attention.

Despite their apparent disdain for adults, most adolescents want and deeply need a mature "significant other." They also need normal activities such as school, work, play, and more responsible social activities. A school program, in fact, is essential when there are enough young people in residence in the hospital. Adolescents have a strong tendency toward grouping, but there exist differing points of view as to whether or not they should be segregated in separate facilities. Integrating them with adult patients, particularly very sick ones, can create problems such as adolescents imitating the adults' very sick behavior or baiting adult patients who may be on their way to a successful recovery. Looking at the other side of the coin, older people can have a stabilizing influence on an adolescent or can become, as individuals, that "significant other" for the troubled teenager.

Although a separate unit for young patients gives them the group-sense they seem to need, it also gives them negative solidarity. In one children's unit, teenagers would frequently "gang up" on an aide who had been left alone during supper hour, steal her keys, lock her in a room, and "escape." This made clear to the administrative staff the need for sufficient evening and weekend coverage. In another unit, a few teenagers would keep the aides occupied with provocative behavior while another group would meet a known "pusher" on the recreation field. Smoking "pot" was a common, though somewhat covert, part of the scene in that particular unit.

Knowledge of drugs, their use, contraindications, and signs of their use should be an integral part of the psychiatric aide's training—whether he is assigned to an adult or an adolescent unit. Drugs and drug abuse have been more fully discussed in Chapter 6.

Overpermissiveness or Overconformity?

There is something charismatic about the aide (or any other member of the staff) who "hits it off" with the adolescent. One factor, however, seems fairly consistent. He neither bends over backward to give in to the incessant demands of his youthful charges, nor does he control them by rigid and punitive means. Neither of these techniques, with few exceptions, can be therapeutically successful. As a matter of fact, this truism could apply in caring for any age group. People simply respond better to a technique which sets limits, though not unreasonable limits, and yet allows for a few instances of letting down the bars—without retribution.

This middle-of-the-road attitude—which should not be lacking in sincere affection—when adhered to uniformly, will work with young people because it engenders trust. Trust is the most significant element that is found lacking in relationships between adolescents and adults, and small wonder. The present generation of middle-aged has given its children little to be trusting about. The promise of a better world which each generation has pledged the next has not come through. Peace is nonexistent, and internal and domestic violence have increased. Because children have "seen everything" on television and movie screens, there is little left to thrill them. When asked if he planned to take his youngsters to the circus, an aide replied: "Kids are too sophisticated today. They're not interested in going. They've seen the circus—every year—on TV." Thus the need to experiment with drugs, dress in a manner that shocks "the establishment," and emulate the violence that is part of their everyday lives.

The adolescent who reaches the psychiatric unit or the community mental health clinic displays (as is the case with his adult counterparts) behavior that offends or is harmful to society or, more often, to himself, and he desperately needs help. Writing in the *National Association of Private Psychiatric Hospitals Journal*, July, 1969, Henry J. Langevin points out: "In addition to specialized and expensive school programs, the needs of the adolescent patients require the expansion of activity programs and higher staffing patterns of nursing personnel, primarily nursing aides."

Remembering that young people are anti-authority, effort should be made to impose controls, but controls that are realistic and can have meaning to them. Aides who have a special interest in younger patients or have special skills to deal with them (and the two really go hand in hand) can be most effective in setting such controls when patients have learned to trust them. Consistency cannot be stressed enough; adolescents can be very seductive, and it is easy to be trapped by pity or over-involvement; it is also easy to be baited into being too strict.

A paragraph from Chapter 8 bears repeating here. "Too much emphasis cannot be laid on the importance of the *attitudes* prevalent on the ward. The importance of the role that the aide plays—whether it be substitute mother, father, sister, brother, friend, teacher, or what—and his mature fulfillment of his patients' needs is vital to his function as a [therapeutic agent] for his patients."

The adolescent patient can be frustrating, aggravating, demanding, unreliable, and a host of other terms we all know. He also can be helped, but not at the expense of other patients. This point should be an important consideration when he is housed with adult patients. Favoritism, on any count, is nontherapeutic, even though we of the adult world may or may not be responsible for the strange and insecure world in which the adolescent finds himself today.

Introduction

*As a seasoned employee who had
learned his job well, he was able to
recognize that there were parts of
his job not to be done with his
hands, and not assigned to him.
These parts of the job were concerned with certain ethical obligations. As the head of a family, as a
confidante bartender, as a co-worker
in other kinds of jobs, he recognized
these ethical obligations immediately. He knew that certain things
were not general information, that
the patient's family was an important part of the patient's total welfare and that he was a part of a
group and thus had to go as the
group went. When he had "bad
days," it threw the group off. Thus,
when troubles arose, he sought his
relief, not through his patients, but
through the offered solutions.*

──────────────────────────14

Your Ethical Obligations

Throughout the course of our daily living, it is essential that we form relationships with other people, either singly, or in groups. The few "hermits" who may be known are frequently classified in psychiatric texts as "simple schizophrenics." We know that they have some emotional maladjustment, for man obviously needs companionship and contact with other men in order to function adequately in his particular culture. Working in a mental hospital, one soon becomes aware that the very sick patient retreats from contact with others; in some areas where patients have been ill for a number of years, a patient will more than likely be completely unaware of his neighbor's name, although he has eaten with him and slept in the same room with him for months on end. Actually, he wants to know and be close to his neighbor, but "running away" has been his defense against hurt for so long that he has forgotten warmth and forgiveness.

Thus, accepting the fact that people need to relate themselves to others, we must also conclude that such relationships are going to be either good or bad, pleasant or unpleasant. One of the most important determinants of the success or the failure of a relationship between two people is *respect*. Respect for the rights, the beliefs and the actions of another person pays him a high compliment. Respect for one's fellow man is fundamental to the successful and comforting care of mental patients. This important feeling is too often lost in a deluge of respect for ourselves—satisfying our own needs and building our own security—unhappily *at the cost of others*. To repeat an old saying: "It is easier to criticize than to try to understand."

No area is looked upon more critically, with more fear and with less understanding than the mental hospital and the unfortunate ill ones who are housed there. Every person working with or around these patients should maintain a fundamental respect for them as human beings and should seize upon every opportunity to tell family, friends, community members, Government officials and so on about this kind of respect and what it means to him. Such telling must be honest and straightforward and sincere; it should be uncolored.

Gossip

About Patients

A bomb can easily wipe out a man's family, his home, his resources and his security. A bit of malicious gossip, dropped here and there, can do exactly the same thing—perhaps not materially but nonetheless with as deadly accuracy and finality. It is a part of daily living to talk about others, since people mingle and work together and become interested in one another to varying degrees.

Occasionally, in a general hospital, personnel are especially cautioned about mentioning the kind of illness or operation that a patient has had. How equally and more important that information about mentally ill patients *never* be revealed except as necessary among those actually working with the patients. Emotional illness is a deeply personal and revealing experience. Events leading up to a mental breakdown often involve not only intimate facts about a patient but also about those persons closest to him—family, friends, business associates. The aide, in his close contact with patients, sees and hears many things which the average, normal person never would admit. His innate respect for his patient should keep him from repeating such matters *anywhere* other than necessary to his job, i.e., reporting to the nurse or the doctor, or in ward conferences regarding patients and the specific care of patients. Recently, an aide was overheard to remark to a patient's mother, "Oh, she's a real problem. They say she masturbates constantly at night!" The horrified mother was not even sure of the meaning of the word and immediately and tearfully related the aide's comment to a group of neighbors. When she found out the true meaning of masturbation she dared not leave the house for days! How unnecessary, how unhelpful for the aide to have made such a remark! How indicative that the aide herself was having difficulties with her own feelings about the patient's masturbating. There is no doubt that there are many times when actions or language or both will shock the aide. However, judgment cannot be passed for the patient since the aide cannot assume that what is wrong for him is equally so for the patient. A patient's behavior is always meaningful *to him*. To feel that he has offended others or will be punished is an undesirable effect resulting from a showing of the aide's own feelings regarding behavior; in other words, it is all right to have such feelings—in fact, it is to be expected—but it is *not* all right to communicate them to the patient. Eventually, he himself must become aware of his undesirable behavior, and this may be a long and painstaking process.

It is inevitable that there will be much "shop talk" among personnel, especially when some workers live on the hospital grounds. It is considered more healthful to find other methods of diversion and other topics of conversation, but when patients are discussed the aide can stop and think: "What am I saying? Is this something that would hurt *me* if I were sick? Is this story any of my business?" Another example of damage resulting from gossip was admitted by an aide to whom it happened. She and another aide were riding home on a crowded streetcar. They were discussing a young boy who had been admitted a few days before. Using his full name, they laughed and joked about his extremely retarded mentality. Then one said to the other, "His brother is P—— H——, the guy who's running for School Board!" A newspaper reporter for the local paper riding behind them on the streetcar summed it up this way: "Potential School Board Director's Brother Reported Insane."

Previously a successful candidate, the man lost the election, and there was little question as to the reason for it.

Mental illness is never a joke, nor should it be treated lightly. The aide knows only too well the heartbreak, the desolate loneliness, the hopeless anger that his patient feels. Remembering this should make confidence his byword.

About Personnel

Because of the very nature of the mental institution—the fact that it is a community in itself—gossip among personnel in inevitable. Technically speaking, the term gossip refers to rumor without any factual basis.

It is perfectly natural for people to talk about one another, since a person is naturally curious about the interests and the background of his friends. Such curiosity is healthful and best satisfied by questioning or feeling out the involved person himself. He is the one who knows the true facts, and it is likely that, in a sincere friendship, he would be willing to reveal any desired information. Unfortunately, many people have not learned to "talk straight" with one another, so that a person often feels it necessary to make up groundless tales about others in order to cover up for that lack of ability. The following true story, taken from an unpublished paper on the subject of gossip, demonstrates how damaging thoughtless remarks can be. A patient walked to the ward office to inquire about his clothing. As he neared the office, he heard one of the aides say, "Where was Dr. S—— last night? We tried to find him when Tom got very upset." The head nurse answered: "Oh! He was probably out somewhere getting drunk, as usual! He's sicker than the patients!" The patient became very disturbed and refused to see Dr. S—— when he came to visit him. He was suspicious of all of the personnel thereafter, and it was a long while before he was able to talk through his fears about being treated by an "alcoholic."

How malicious gossip can be, and how quickly and easily a simple bit of information can grow and twist, is illustrated by another example. An aide had become involved in some difficulty with the police in his home town nearby. They asked him to drive to court with them, and he was released from duty to go. Within a very short time the story was all over the hospital that "Mr. A—— had to be dragged out of the building by six policemen." Actually, he had walked out quickly accompanied by one detective in plain clothes!

Gossip is sometimes used as a method of "getting even." This is particularly true when there is a lot of feeling among personnel concerning authority. The person whose job it is to direct others, from the charge aide on up, is often the victim of considerable gossip. More often than not such stories are circulated merely to lower the individual in the eyes of others.

Thus, the aide who would not wish his own name bandied about in a mesh of untruths can think twice before talking about his co-workers and others; he can remember that he does not always know the facts and that what he says can go a long way toward really hurting another person.

Patients' Records

Each hospital has its own regulations concerning who may or may not read patients' complete records. There are also two schools of thought as to the actual value of reading records; those who think that it is helpful in the care of patients, and those who think that it creates unnecessary prejudices. Whatever the system or the opinion, a patient's record contains a multitude of information concerning his past, present and future *personal* life. That factor is usually responsible for the fact that sometimes records are kept separate from the ward and frequently under lock and key. Obviously, personal information about patients must be kept confidential. Actually, when the aide considers how he would *feel* if he were a patient and knew that everything about him was common knowledge, he would be much less likely to reveal the contents of patient's records than he might otherwise do.

There is another important point to be remembered, and that is that a patient's record (and, as a matter of fact, the record of any *employee*) is considered to be legal evidence and can be used as such in judicial matters.

Revealing anything contained in a patient's record anywhere other than in the necessary course of duty can do as much damage as ruthless gossip.

The Patient's Family

The aide often sees the relatives of patients more frequently than any other member of the staff. Thus, it is extremely important that the aide understand the patient's family and what they mean to the patient. The aide has an important responsibility to record his observation of patients with their families, and also patient's reactions before and after visits.

Patient's families appear to be very difficult and trying, particularly at first, and will spend much time in constant questioning, possible accusation of personnel and impatience with the patient. The reasons for this behavior are fairly simple: the relatives feel guilty about having had to place their loved one in a mental hospital (about which they have undoubtedly heard all the usual terrible things); they are afraid, because they do not understand mental illness, and thus do not really know how to behave; they feel altogether helpless, since they have been unable to handle the problem at home and they cannot seem to see their own part in the patient's illness.

Often, relatives are a trial because they insist on breaking hospital rules and regulations. For example, time after time they will leave matches with patients who are on admission wards. Sometimes they bring food to a patient who is part of a special study or is on a special diet. An aide recently asked: "What are we going to do on our ward? There must be a dozen of our patient's relatives who insist on giving them matches, even though we have requested many times that they refrain from doing so." This poses a difficult problem. However, it may help to list those relatives who refuse to pay any attention to regulations and give the list to the doctor. Possibly, he can make clear to relatives the very good reasons for restricting matches or food.

The aide's major responsibility to the patient's family is, of course, to take the best possible care of him. Along with that basic duty, questions concerning the patient's illness should be referred to the doctor, and discussion of the patient's ward behavior should be as limited as possible. Best care of the patient includes the assurance that his personal possessions will be carefully checked—particularly clothing—and that personal possessions do not get lost. If clothing, pocketbooks, radios, books, and such items are accurately listed on the patient's clothing card *as each is received,* there should be little danger of loss through carelessness. Loss through destructiveness or wearing should also be noted in the same place, and relatives should be told about it on their next visit after the loss.

Much can be done by the aide by means of simple, quiet reassurance. Telling about the good supper a patient ate the night before, or of his interest in baseball games on the television set, or what an expert he is getting to be at ping-pong, all serve to make the family more comfortable about his hospitalization.

Relatives can be most useful in terms of bringing patients small needed items (a comb or tobacco or some sewing materials or magazines), and in accepting times when their visits are most helpful and desired. Aides frequently can form effective friendships with relatives and can extend their public relations job through educational contact with the patient's family.

Accepting money or gifts from patient's relatives given expressly in the hope that it will provide special care or attention for a particular patient is not morally right. With 25 to 50 patients for whom to care, how can an aide, or any other employee, give special care or attention to only one? And if this *is* done for one, what happens to the rest?

Channels

Most institutions, especially large ones, are like any other organization and are set up administratively into departments. Each department has a head person and some assistants whose job it is to organize and direct the department and "keep the wheels going." It goes without saying that direction is needed, as for example, in the distribution of supplies. Somebody has to order supplies in bulk; somebody else has to sort them and get items together according to size, material, and so on; and somebody else has to deliver them to a designated place. Another example is the nursing service where someone has to know when personnel vacancies exist; someone must do the hiring to fill the vacancies; someone must provide coverage for vacations and sick leave; someone must handle personnel problems, supply problems and a hundred other things.

The director of a department must have assistants, and these assistants must have other assistants because no one person could possibly handle all of the problems arising each day in a large organization. Although the major responsibility of all employees of a mental hospital "from the top down" is to provide the best possible care for patients, the welfare of personnel is almost equally important. Personnel who are dissatisfied with their placement or want special time off or need help of one sort or another want ways to answer their problems.

Accomplishing a task by working through those persons best able to assist is known as "proceeding through channels." The primary purpose of requiring that personnel proceed through channels is to distribute the load of work more evenly among those "directing operations." For example, an aide complains to the head nurse that there are not enough sheets to ensure clean beds for his patients. The head nurse, who knows that her regular quota will not provide more, calls the supervisor. The supervisor may have a reserve supply to draw from, but if not, she must call the head of the linen room or the laundry to request a special issue of sheets. This may seem like a lot of unnecessary detail, but actually it keeps everyone informed about what is going on, makes urgent needs *known* to those who should know them. For example, linen would disappear by the carload were there not a system for its circulation.

Another very common illustration of disregard for channels is as follows: an aide wants special days off. Instead of approaching the head nurse or the supervisor whose job it is to make out the time and to provide proper coverage, he sees the director of nurses. Theoretically, the director should communicate with the supervisor to determine the advisability of granting the particular aide special time off, but should she neglect to do this and grant the time, all kinds of morale problems arise. The supervisor feels that she is not trusted or supported by the director; the head nurse may have to work without sufficient help; and other aides will complain over favoritism and the necessity for their doing extra work.

The simplest way for the aide to get the things he needs, or to find out the things he wants to know is *first* to consult the person closest to the situation and to let him "carry the ball" from there. When everybody knows what is going on, things generally run more smoothly.

Obligations Toward the Job

When a person comes to work in a hospital, the first and foremost thing of which he always must be aware is the fact that *a hospital,* unlike most other organizations *runs 24 hours a day, 7 days a week!* It is well to be perfectly aware of this in the beginning, since it *does* make differences in one's obligations toward the job. For instance, it means working weekends and working different shifts. It means that 21 meals a week have to be prepared, served, and cleaned up after; it means that cleanliness is as necessary at 3 or 5 o'clock in the morning as it is at 1 o'clock in the afternoon. In a mental hospital it means that bathing and dressing apply not only to oneself each day but to a number of other people too. It *should* mean that there is much more to work for each week than a paycheck.

It has been said many times in this text that mental hospitals suffer acutely from personnel shortages. There are not nearly enough positions provided for the proper care of patients. Thus, any absence, due to illness or for other reasons, creates a serious gap in the amount of work that can be done. An aide working in a mental hospital is obligated to maintain good health, and if an aide is unfortunate enough to contract an illness which leaves him unable to meet the full obligations of his job, he should seek other, less taxing work. For example, aides will return to work after a major operation and report that they can do no lifting or pulling, or that they are unable to climb stairs or walk long distances. It is most certainly the employer's obligation to help that person find a job less strenuous than aide work, but if the aide insists on staying, it creates almost as serious a shortage as an actual vacancy. There is no ward in the mental hospital in which some lifting or pulling, stair-climbing or walking is not an absolute necessity. Vacation and sick leave policies are provided so that personnel can maintain good health. Most hospitals provide clinic services for personnel. Aides are well aware of what it is like to have to do "double work"—that is, to do his own and someone else's work when his co-worker is absent and no relief person is available. This does not mean to imply that an employee should try to work when he is legitimately ill, or that it is his fault that he has a heart attack or a serious operation; on the contrary, it only means that it is always hoped that the employee thinks enough of his patients, his co-workers and *his* hospital to be able to recognize when he is able to work to his full capacity and when he is not. The aide may say: "What can I do? This is the only experience I have had!" But what an experience! It should develop one's capacity for understanding human behavior, one's ability to meet people successfully, and many sedentary jobs insist on these two factors above all else! Receptionists, companions for older people, children's nurses, taxicab drivers—all these require patience, understanding and the capacity to relate oneself to others.

Usually, aides are requested to "call the office" when they are ill or know that they are going to be late. The reason for this request is quite simple; if the supervisor knows about illness or tardiness, an attempt can be made *ahead of time* to provide relief. Similarly, if an aide has found a better job, plans to leave the state, is pregnant, or wants to go to school, at least two weeks' notice of resignation should be given so that a replacement may be found *before* the aide leaves.

Some of the obligations which are not so obvious are involved with the fact that an aide is a member of a *group*. As such, he is expected to do his share of the work, to limit his talk about others to *facts*, to offer constructive suggestions where they will do the most good and to separate, as much as possible, his personal feelings from his job.

The aide *owes it to himself* to try to forget his job as much as he can when he is away from it. It is a strenuous enough proposition to begin with, both mentally and physically, without carrying it home with him.

Sometimes, personnel are asked to relieve in a ward other than their own, or they may be asked to stay overtime for a special occasion or an emergency. An aide is not asked to do this because he is being "picked on." If there is no good reason for such a request the matter needs looking into, but ordinarily it is made as a last resort and because no other remedy can be found.

To sum it all up, if the job means more to the aide than his paycheck, if it means the safety and the well-being of his patients and the teamwork of the group as a whole, then he has assumed his obligations and is worthy of the tribute which is so rightly his—that the aide is the arms and the legs and the backbone of the mental hospital!

Your Personal Problems

All of us have personal problems—some large and some small. We need to feel that someone is interested and that someone *cares*. The aide has a difficult job, and sometimes he has difficulties at home or in other personal areas with which he would like some help. Theoretically, the mental hospital can offer help with almost any problem and should be willing to do so. The least that can be done is referral to the proper person or agency that can make things easier. Many examples come to mind. The aide who has problems with drinking can be counseled regarding Alcoholics Anonymous or alcoholic clinics; an aide with financial difficulties can be advised as to his safest contact for a loan to tide things over; an aide with emotional difficulties can be referred by the clinic doctor to a mental health clinic, or a specific therapist; and aide having interpersonal difficulties in his ward should be able to discuss them with his supervisor so that steps can be taken to remedy the situation.

The important point is that there are ways of being helped with personal problems, and it should not be necessary merely to continue to live with them. Many dangers lie hidden in such a stalemate. Most serious is the probability that personal problems will be inflicted on patients, and this should be avoided at all cost. The patient is, after all, a sick person needing help, and most times incapable of offering help or solace. Transferring problems to patients does not necessarily mean sitting down and telling a patient about personal difficulties. It is usually not so obvious. However, it is true that we do "take out our feelings" on patients in many ways. Sometimes, we are not aware of it. Under personal stress we may speak sharply to them or force them to do something they do not wish to do, or we are depressed around them, and they feel it. How much better if we work out our personal feelings in other ways and on other people who can help us and will not be hurt by things done that are not really meant to be harmful.

An acquaintance, an administrator, has often said: "When things get real tough, when everything seems to be going wrong, and I have listened to all the problems I can stand,

I have a remedy. Instead of taking out my tension and frustration on my secretary or my assistants, I start walking toward the farthest patient building on the grounds. I start there, and I go through several buildings, sitting awhile with the patients, listening to them, or watching part of a TV show with them. Some of them are so sick and so forlorn, and their needs are so great that I soon become ashamed of my own intolerance. I go back to work with renewed spirits. In this way I don't take out my feelings on anybody. I only have to look and listen, and my own feelings are dissolved."

Introduction

Many nights, in his quarters, the main topic of the "bull sessions" was concern for the future. He knew that he wanted to continue this work for some time to come, perhaps even as a lifework, but he wondered about his chances for advancement and his chances for further education. He and his friends talked a great deal about the status of aides throughout the country and kept up with news about national organizations which were working toward betterment of the aides' working conditions and toward proper recognition of their valuable contributions in the care of the mentally ill.

What did the future hold for him and for thousands of his fellow workers?

---------------------------------15

Looking Ahead With You

Over the past decade the chances for psychiatric aides to gain opportunities from their employment and education to move up the career ladder have improved considerably. Whereas at one time the aide or community mental health worker could look forward to only minimal promotion, today there is actually no real limit to keep him from going as far as he wants to go.

One of the largest factors which has influenced this change in outlook has been the influence of aides themselves. Relatively few professionals—physicians, nurses, social workers and others who have made psychiatry and mental health their careers—have taken a real interest, that is, a sustained interest, in this very large group of workers who have contributed so much toward the care of the mentally sick or potentially mentally sick.

In some states aides have organized, set up training and education standards, and have insisted on—and gotten— licensure. Some of these groups have dropped the term "aide" and call themselves psychiatric technicians.

With the extension of psychiatry into the community, opportunities are available for mental health workers, including aides, to become "patient advocates," "rehabilitative aides," "mental health aides" or whatever the community mental health center calls its nonprofessional workers. Since the focus is on the home and the community and the emphasis is on prevention, the mental health aide often provides the "in" between the professionals and the clients. Very often he has lived through some of the very frustrations the people in the community are enduring; he may be similar to prospective clients in background, way of life, educational level, language and so on.

Motivation

Most people who have to work for a living do so with a set goal in mind. This goal is concerned primarily with advancement, with getting ahead. Advancement does not only mean making more money, although that is necessarily an important consideration in this day and age, but it also means gaining prestige and *recognition* for a job well done. Anyone who puts forth sincere effort resulting in production usually can achieve his goal eventually. The mental hospital aide who can recall the patients on his ward who have gotten well or have at least made a better hospital adjustment will know that he has had a large part in a rapidly progressing movement to combat our greatest health problem. The community mental health worker also can recall his success in averting a crisis at home or in convincing a client to come to the center for help.

Actually, progress in helping that vast group of human beings who are mentally ill is only beginning. For hundreds of years there has been mental sickness, and for hundreds of years people have tried to find ways of caring for mental sickness. Some of the efforts have been valuable and helpful. Others have done equally as much to destroy any good which has been accomplished.

During the past 25 years, for the first time in history, energy has been consistently directed toward improvement, toward finding the best answers to the innumerable questions still unanswered regarding care, treatment and cure of mental illness.

Mental health aides constitute the largest group of workers contributing to the care of mentally ill people. Realistically, psychiatrists, nurses and other groups are so outnumbered by patients that they could not begin to care for their patients without the help of these aides.

The aide is an important member of the mental hospital team. It is the aide who maintains for his patients an atmosphere which encourages the regaining of good health, who helps the nurse in carrying out treatment plans for the patient, who is right at hand for 24 hours daily to meet the needs, great and small, of thousands of sick people.

The aide's contribution, then, becomes vital and necessary and will continue to be so for many years to come. Take, for example, an average day in a fairly well-staffed mental hospital. Much goes on: there are various treatments to be given, several dozen patients get individual or group therapy, x-rays and laboratory specimens are taken, perhaps one or two operations are performed, religious services are held, and groups of patients may go on picnics. *Without aides, much of this routine could not be completed.* By 5 o'clock in the afternoon, the "bosses" have gone home, social service workers, occupational therapists, psychologists and technicians have gone off duty, there is a doctor "on call," and perhaps the chaplain. But *the wheels do not stop.* Patients have their supper, perhaps they see a movie, they go to bed, and if sleep is impossible, there is someone to talk to, someone to give them a snack. That someone is the aide.

The future holds much promise for the hospital aide who is faithful and does his job well. An aide who alone cares for 45 untidy, senile and very sick patients each day from 2:30 in the afternoon to 11 o'clock at night recently said: "I am so discouraged. Week in and week out I work here in this ward for a few dollars a week, and nobody *cares* one way or another." This aide is mistaken. More than *anyone,* his patients care—very much—and their families care. Actually, the "bosses" care, too, and are constantly working to improve conditions for him and countless other aides. The problem is *not* that "nobody cares"—it is that far too often people do not let the aide *know* that they care. The job is so big, and there are so many obstacles that visible appreciation for such courage and effort sometimes gets lost in the overwhelming task of keeping the ball rolling.

Humane, sincere, and consistent effort will be rewarded. This is the aide's and mental health worker's place in the scheme of things. Motivation for the psychiatric aide is also found in the opportunities for which his job prepares him. He has learned to work with people, to understand behavior. He has had to learn to organize his work, to use economically the time available for accomplishing large tasks. He has learned to think and to plan, and he has learned to follow directions. Thus, if his future does not include a career of mental health work, he is at least better prepared by virtue of his experiences as an aide to pursue whatever other work he has chosen. Many doctors worked their way through medical school as psychiatric aides. Aides have gone into social service work, nursing, psychology, occupational therapy, and other related fields.

Some aides with families or other obligations are content to work steadily in the mental hospital and to make a career out of caring for the mentally ill. Most hospitals provide adequate security for the future for such workers, and it is hardly necessary to point out their very real contribution to society.

Further Education

In talking with aides who have had an inservice course in their own hospital, one immediately determines that, for most of them, this is not enough. In fact, it is only the beginning. More and more aides express the desire to go further educationally to improve their knowledge and to carry such improvement back to their jobs.

In many areas of the country, courses for aides have been developed and are being offered to interested persons. These courses differ regarding the length of time involved, the content offered and their points of emphasis (i.e., some courses are more concerned with procedures and techniques; others follow the general pattern of the basic nursing course; still others are geared to the so-called "dynamic" approach). Whatever the pattern, the aide can and should obtain accurate advice from the proper, qualified persons as to which course to take. He should know what he wants, what is his ultimate goal and which course most readily meets his desires and for which he is best qualified.

Some universities offer cooperative plans in conjunction with mental hospitals or mental health clinics. An aide may enroll in such a plan which provides for so many weeks of university work and so many weeks of on-the-job experience.

An aide with a satisfactory high school record and experience in mental health work may wish to apply for full-time university work which eventually will earn for him a degree in the field in which he is most interested.

Many aides, because of family responsibilities or for other reasons, may not be able to afford to go on to a college or a university. They are finding it to their advantage to attend a school of practical nursing. In 1968, there were 1,191 such state-approved programs in the United States (and Puerto Rico). Following completion of the program, licensure is provided for in all states and is relatively permissive.* In 1968, 36 states had mandatory licensure laws, but again,

---

* Facts About Nursing, 10 Columbus Circle, New York City, American Nurses' Association, edition 1969.

these laws are relatively permissive. Thus, it seems advisable for aides who wish to make a career of hospital work, whether in a mental hospital or other type of health facility, to attain licensure as a practical nurse.

Scholarship aid from state and federal funds is becoming more and more accessible to qualified applicants. Of course, the aide should select an approved program. Most of the practical nurse programs take 12 months, although in some states it takes longer.

Obviously, the aide who has had previous experience working in a mental hospital will benefit considerably more from a practical nursing program than the person who has had no hospital experience at all.

New Careers

During the later part of the 1960's and the early 1970's, more and more educators, writers, and professionals in the mental health field have voiced the conviction that further career opportunities must be made available to nonprofessional workers. Many advocate the "career ladder" though there are variations in how to program such a ladder.

The National Institute of Mental Health, Continuing Education Program of the Division of Manpower and Training, is now offering potential mental health workers regular assistance at any public or private nonprofit educational institution. The psychiatric technician program in the state of California offers mental health aides the opportunity to become licensed and to move on to junior college degrees. An example of this type of program at the Porterville (California) College requires "completion of high school or equivalent" for admission and offers a 50-week program consisting of 10 hours of classes per week at the college and 22 hours of clinical training. Successful trainees earn 50 semester units of college credit, and are eligible to take the licensing examination of the California Department of Professional and Vocational Standards, Board of Vocational Nurse and Psychiatric Technician Examiners. The Porterville College brochure goes on to say: "It is possible to obtain the associate of arts degree by completing an additional 12 units of required courses." Other states have similar programs.

The Southern Regional Education Board has for the past several years promoted Community College Mental Health Worker programs in the South. In January, 1969, 18 colleges that participated in Atlanta in a workshop on curriculum development reported that they include mental retardation courses as part of their required curricula. The colleges, offering a two-year program to develop mental health workers, are attempting to provide a program that can be integrated with four-year institutions so that graduates can continue their mental health careers.

There is still a severe shortage of programs, however, and more must be developed to meet some of the serious manpower shortages in both community mental health centers and various types of mental hospitals in this country. The development of career ladders—of whatever kind—is essential to these programs and the capable, motivated mental health worker must be encouraged—and materially assisted—to start the career ladder climb.

In some states, tuition is paid and educational leave granted to aides so that they can take college courses, but such opportunities must be further liberalized and educational programs expanded.

It is probably admittedly true that not very many aides starting at the "lowest level" in the mental hospital or community mental health center will be able to make the long climb to a top position. But it *is* possible, and some exceptional aides do end up with doctorates—still working for the betterment of the mentally ill. Only a few weeks ago I received a letter from a man who reminded me that a number of years ago, while making rounds on the night shift, I had caught him (at that time, a psychiatric aide) sleeping on duty. The initials after his name on that letter were "Ph.D."

Job Opportunities

The concentration throughout this text has been on the hospital psychiatric aide and the community mental health worker. There are also excellent job opportunities developing in the realm of nursing homes and in the area of mental retardation, particularly in the latter as what Burmeister calls "professional houseparents" or "cottage parents."* Burmeister also uses these terms to describe workers who live in cottages with disturbed children and adolescents.

There are new roles opening up, too, in both hospitals and mental health centers. Professionals are finally beginning to accept psychiatric aides as group and individual therapists (a role many of them have carried out informally for years). According to a small study done by Pasewark and others: "Patients hospitalized in a state mental hospital were interviewed to determine their opinions concerning the ward aide as a group and individual therapist. In general, this idea was received quite favorably by patients, who also expressed the opinion that the aide would prove a more effective [individual] therapist than some of the more highly trained professional groups employed by a mental hospital."†

The mental health worker-psychiatric aide can be a youth counselor, a "patient advocate," a home visitor, or a liaison between the sometimes "distant" professional and a particular ethnic group. Administrators and professionals must pay more attention to advancing those aides who show capability, apti-

---

* Burmeister, Eva: The Professional Houseparent, New York, Columbia University Press, 1960.

† Pasewark, R. A., *et al.*: The mental hospital patient's perception of the aide as psychotherapist, *Journal of Psychiatric Nursing and Mental Health Services,* Vol. 8, No. 1, p. 29, Jan.-Feb., 1970.

tude, and a desire to advance themselves—*and ultimately be more effective with patients.*

Frank Reissman (see bibliography), who has probably done more for the "new careers" concept than anyone else—particularly among the disadvantaged—writes: "It appears that a much greater investment in education, health, welfare, and recreation is projected for [this] decade than was indicated three or four years ago. And further investment in these areas must strain already overdrawn resources. The solution can only come through changing the nature of the service (health, education, and welfare) through more efficient use of highly-trained personnel supplemented by cadres of less highly-trained staff."*

The increased responsibilities which the prepared psychiatric aide and the community mental health worker is assuming and will continue to assume eventually will enforce the status, the salary and the recognition which he so rightfully deserves.

Your Unique Contribution

The unique contribution which is made by the aide in the daily, tremendous job of caring for the mentally ill is *his closeness to the patient.* Throughout this text, it has been pointed out again and again that the courage, the hard work and the faithfulness of the aide have been and are the mainstay of the mental institutions of this country. The emerging role of community mental health workers, too, is fast becoming a mainstay in mental health centers and clinics, particularly in the widely diverse urban ghetto areas and rural communities of this nation.

In my consistently held opinion, there is no doubt that the future holds the prominent recognition for these workers which is so rightfully theirs.

---

* Pearl, Arthur, and Reissman, Frank: New Careers for the Poor, p. 247, New York, The Free Press, 1965.

———Appendix A

Definitions

Addiction: Complete dependence on a drug (including alcohol). A person will go to any lengths to obtain the drug.

Affect: A feeling which becomes engulfing and constant. A "mood" that stays with a person.

Aggression: The need to push oneself forward, usually hostilely by word or action.

Ambivalence: Opposite feelings (i.e., love and hate) existing at the same time toward a person or object.

Anorexia: Lack of appetite.

Anxious: Feeling of tension because of a real or imagined danger.

Autistic thinking: Daydreaming, self-centered.

Blocking: A sudden stopping in thought, word, or action. Usually indicates anxiety or conflict.

Catalepsy: Waxlike posture that may be maintained for a long time.

Compulsion: An unshakable impulse to act against one's better judgment.

Conflict: An uncomfortable, even painful, feeling resulting from the presence of opposing desires.

Confusion: A state of puzzlement. Lack of clear thinking. Usually not well oriented.

Delusion: A fixed, false idea. No amount of reasoning changes the (patient's) idea. (For example, delusions of grandeur: "I am Queen Anne," or "I am the Governor of this state." Delusions of persecution: "I was put here by gangsters," or "You're all F.B.I. members out to get me.")

Depression: An unshakable feeling of sadness.

Deterioration: A progressive failure of the intellectual processes.

239

Appendix A

Dynamic: In psychiatry it means an interest in people that extends beyond a description of behavior to the "why" people behave as they do.

Ego: The ego is the portion of our personality that has to make the decisions. It says "I will" or "I will not." Most of the ego is conscious and represents the thinking, knowing, feeling part of a person.

Emotion: A strong feeling, usually in relation to people.

Empathy: A feeling of sympathetic communication with another person or group.

Euphoria: A magnified feeling of well-being.

Exhibitionism: Exposure of the body or the sex organs or actions to attract sexual interest.

Flight of ideas: Changing rapidly from one subject to another without ever reaching the point.

Hallucination: A sensory perception without actual stimulus (i.e., seeing, hearing, feeling, etc., something when, to all appearances nothing is there).

Heterosexual: Sexual attraction toward persons of the opposite sex.

Homosexual: Sexual attraction toward persons of the same sex.

Id: The "primitive" part of the mind that implements what one *wants* to do as opposed to what one should do.

Illusion: A sensory perception with actual stimulus (i.e., a spot on the wall may become a spider, or the wind sighing in the trees may become a voice calling).

Insight: Awareness and acceptance of oneself and one's problems.

Masturbation: Self-manipulation to arouse sexual feelings.

Mental (defense) mechanisms: Ways of thinking, usually followed by action, which serve to meet personal needs.

Motor activity: Activity involving bodily movement.

Narcissism: Love of self; the person considers his own body as the love object.

Negativism: General resistance to any outside suggestion (i.e., patients who will not bathe, eat, etc., when such activity is suggested by others).

Obsession: An unshakable urge to think thoughts that one does not wish to think.

Perversion: Usually refers to abnormal sexual acts.

Phantasy: Day dreaming. Building for oneself things which do not exist in one's real situation.

Phobia: An exaggerated, morbid fear of something (of high places, crowds, dirt, etc.).

Regression: A person's behavior becomes very infantile and withdrawn (i.e., the patient who wants to play with dolls; the "untidy" patient).

Rejection: A refusal to accept a person or a thing.

Repression: A defense mechanism used to keep from consciousness unpleasant experiences or ideas.

Retardation: Slowing up of reactions (i.e., slowness of movements or thought processes).

Sublimation: A defense mechanism used to change unacceptable desires into constructive actions.

Suggestibility: Easy acceptance of the suggestions of others for action or thought.

Superego: The "conscience"—that which controls what one *should* do to comply with social "norms."

Suppression: A conscious holding back of unpleasant thoughts or actions.

Transference Unconscious identification with another person who assumes the role of an individual with whom the patient has had previous experience.

Unconscious: Mental activity of which an individual is not aware, but which affects behavior.

———Appendix B

Reading List

History of Mental Illness:

Armiger, Sister Bernadette: The History of the Hospital Work of the Daughters of Charity of St. Vincent De Paul in the Eastern Province of the United States 1823-1860 (unpublished Master's dissertation, 1947, available on interlibrary loan from the Catholic University of America, Washington, D.C.).

Beers, C.: A Mind That Found Itself: An Autobiography (with supplement on the mental hygiene movement), rev. ed., New York, Doubleday, 1948.

Deutsch, A.: The Mentally Ill in America: A History of Their Care and Treatment from Colonial Times, New York, Columbia University Press, 1949.

Growth and Development:

English, O. S., and Pearson, G. H. J.: The Emotional Problems of Living, Avoiding the Neurotic Pattern, 3rd ed., New York, Norton, 1963.

Psychiatric Nursing:

Matheney, R., and Topalis, M.: Psychiatric Nursing, 5th ed., St. Louis, C. V. Mosby, 1970.

Mereness, D., and Karnosh, L.: Essentials of Psychiatric Nursing, St. Louis, C. V. Mosby, 1963.

Orlando Ida, J.: Dynamic Nurse-Patient Relationship, Putnam, New York, 1961.

Robinson, A. M.: Communicating with schizophrenic patients, Am. J. Nurs. 60:1120-1123, August, 1960.

Travelbee, J.: Interpersonal Aspects of Nursing, Philadelphia, F. A. Davis, 1966.

Mental Retardation:

McClelland, L. H.: Textbook for Psychiatric Technicians, St. Louis, C. V. Mosby, 1967.

Peterson, L. W.: Operant approach to observation and recording, Nurs. Outlook 15:28-32, March, 1967.

————: Operant learning theory; a framework deserving nursing investigation, Nurs. Res. 15:229-235, Summer, 1966.

Tredgold, R. R., and Soddy, K.: Textbook of Mental Deficiency, 11th ed., Baltimore, Williams & Wilkins, 1970.

Pharmacology and Drug Abuse:

Drug Abuse: Escape to Nowhere, available from Smith, Kline and French Laboratories, 1500 Spring Garden St., Philadelphia, Pa.

Drug Abuse in Adolescents. Report of the Committee on Youth, American Academy of Pediatrics, Pediatrics, 44:131-141, July, 1969.

Goodman, L. S., and Gilman, A.: The Pharmacologic Basis of Therapeutics, 3rd ed., New York, Macmillan, 1965

Douglas, F. N.: Pharmacology and Clinical Nursing, New York, Appleton-Century-Crofts, 1970.

Rodman, M. J., and Smith, D. W.: Pharmacology and Drug Therapy in Nursing, Philadelphia, J. B. Lippincott, 1968.

Basic Nursing Care:

Johnson, D. F.: Total Patient Care: Foundations and Practice, 2nd ed., St. Louis, C. V. Mosby, 1968.

Keane, C. B.: Essentials of Nursing; a Medical-Surgical Text for Practical Nurses, 2nd ed., Philadelphia, W. B. Saunders, 1969.

Blanton, S.: Love or Perish, expanded ed., New York, Simon & Schuster, 1957.

Smith, D. W., Germain, C. P. H., and Gips, C. D.: Care of the Adult Patient, 3rd ed., Philadelphia, J. B. Lippincott, 1971.

Classification of Mental Illness:

Diagnostic and Statistical Manual of Mental Disorders, 3rd ed., American Psychiatric Association, 1700 18th Street, N.W., Washington, D.C., 20009, $3.50.

Community Mental Health:

Dupont, H.: Community mental health centers and services for the mentally retarded, Community Ment. Health J. 3:1: 33-36, Spring, 1967.

The Comprehensive Community Mental Health Center, an annotated bibliography. Public Health Service Publication No. 1980, available from the Superintendent of Documents, U.S. Government Printing Office, Washington, D.C., 20402, 30¢.

Gorman, M.: Models of Delivery of Mental Health Services to the Community in the 1970's, available from National Committee Against Mental Illness, 1028 Connecticut Ave., N.W., Washington, D.C., 20036, 10¢.

New Careers and Aide Training:

Attendant Training in Southern Residential Facilities for the Mentally Retarded, Report of the Southern Regional Educational Board Attendant Training Project, Southern Regional Education Board, 130 Sixth St., Atlanta Ga. 30300.

Highlights from Survey of Psychiatric Aides, U.S. Department of Health, Education and Welfare, Public Health Service. Public Health Service Publication No. 1151, available from the Superintendent of Documents, U.S. Government Printing Office, Washington, D.C., 20402, 20¢.

Burmeister, E.: The Professional Houseparent, New York, Columbia University Press, 1960.

Pearl, A., and Reissman, F.: New Careers for the Poor, New York, The Free Press, 1965.

Reissman, F.: Strategies Against Poverty, New York, Random House, 1969.

Pasewark, R. A., Hall, W. T., and Grice, J. E., Jr.: The mental hospital patient's perception of the aide as a psychotherapist, J. Psychiat. Nurs. and Ment. Health Serv. 8:1:29, Jan.-Feb., 1970.

Of Special Interest:

Facts About Mental Illness 1970, The National Association for Mental Health, Inc., 10 Columbus Circle, New York, N.Y. 10019.

Joint Commission on Mental Illness and Health: Action for Mental Health (Final Report), New York, Basic Books, 1961.

Robinson, A. M.: Remotivation Technique (newest edition has application to nursing homes), available from the American Psychiatric Association, 1700 18th Street, N.W., Washington, D.C., 20009.

Schwartz, M. S., and Schwartz, C. B.: Social Approaches to Mental Patient Care, Final Report of the Task Force on Patterns of Patient Care established by the Joint Commission on Mental Illness and Health, New York, Columbia University Press, 1964.

Index

Index